To everyone who has ever been lost only to find themself even closer to home.

To YOU who has drawn this book into your reality, may it inspire you to think bigger than ever: to help YOU become even more you.

In gratitude and love, xxx

Josephine

"When love walks into your life we answer"

With all my love & gratitude

Josephine

For my parents Gini and Flemming without whom I would not be who I am today. For my loving partner Craig without whose support I would not have found myself in the inredible way I did. And for my wonderful siblings Tobias, Oliver and Silke each of you makes me a better me.

To all my loved souls all around the world and beyond,

Forever grateful to you all.

The 30 Day Morning Miracle

Introduction

Hello you who picked up this book. I am SO happy to meet you here on the page. I have been waiting for YOU to come along for a really long time (trust me at times I had nearly given up hope but then I remembered that you were simply lost in the world of being a busy human being doing what most other humans do these days: rush around to forget all about their dreams and aspirations).

So my love, you see how much I appreciate that YOU decided to make a difference? Before we get started I want you to know that this is no coincedence that YOU picked up this book today of all days!! Not that anything is ever a coincedence but we will get to that in another book;) YOU are here for a reason and the knowledge you will gain through EXPERIENCING this book (yes not reading!) will dramatically transform your life into one that is in full alignment with that which is in your heart.

Take a moment to breathe, it's a lot to take in I know: breathe in faith, hold it, exhale out doubt hold it. Repeat a few more times until you feel only your heart beating and singing with JOY and remembrance.

Good, now let's get to work:

As you have chosen me to be your guide it seems only fair that you should know my name so let me introduce myself to you, however be warned: Im bold and to the point so try and keep your mind quiet and your heart open as you continue to read on:

My name is Josephine McGrail and I have been seeking you my whole life. I have travelled all across the planet to find you and I am so happy to know that we have finally met. It is my soul's calling you see: I am a intuitive healer which means I work with the energy that we as humans can't see or touch, only feel through the gateway of the heart. When you are I are in alignment magic happens, you have felt it yourself many times in your life: when the entire Universe seems to align and flow with you: a bus arrives exactly when you need it, a thought appears just as someone asks you about that specific subject, a last minute gut instinct to take a different route to the airport saves you missing your flight, following your intuition to change job meant you met your wonderful partner etc etc.

That's the Universe gently whispering into your ears at night. Reminding you who you are.

They say it takes 30 days to change or create a habit. That's all good you think: Thats wayyyy too long for me! I know what I want and I want it NOW. As in ASAP!!

That's all possible my love; Im RIGHT here with you, backing you up, cheering you on, continually encouraging YOU even when the going gets (a little) tough.

For what they dont tell you is that you, just like EVERYBODY else who really wants to transform, are going to need support. FUCK.

But NO: this is awesome news: means we are all in this together. And that ONLY by opening UP to our surroundings can, and WILL we succeed in ANY endeavour you seek to fulfil.

Im not here to give you the BIG words about how it will happen, or huge inspirational stories about my own journey (come see me for a tea if that's what you really wanna hear about). We: YOU and I, are going to keep this really simple:

Every morning for 30 days we are going to connect first thing every day (yep that means getting up a lil earlier YIKES;).

YOU are going to PLAN your day by tuning into how YOU are feeling.

YOU are going to get INSPIRATION from ME about how to align with your deepest and highest desires.

YOU are going to take action.

I AM going to cheer you on. ALL THE WAY.

The next morning we repeat.

That's IT!!! No long texts to get confused about. No fuzz. No frills.

Just YOU & ME babe.

Simple.

NOW LETS BEGIN

YOU GOT THIS

xxx Love Josephine

Day 1 New beginnings

Good morning my love,

YEAHHH you are IN!!!! FAB!!! I AM so crazy excited because I know what you don't know (yet) that YOU are a WINNER!

NO way you would have picked up this book, read the intro and even DECIDED to INVEST energy and time in your own happiness if that wasn't so. FACT.

I wish you a fantastic day ahead and remember TODAY, more than ever before, you have an opportunity to start a fresh. A New Beginning... So let go of whatever took place before that made you feel small; yesterday, last year- the past has no power over you if you don't allow it too.
Remember that which we focus on grows!! So today, now more than ever before, look for NEW BEGINNINGS; new people, new ideas, new places and spaces (including all materialistic as well as energetic) that LIFTS YOUR ENERGY & YOUR HEART: FEEL into you...

Remember who you are BECOMING.
I believe in YOU 100000000%

Now let's begin our day with our morning ritual:
Commit to doing it FIRST thing when you wake up- before anything else!
Why?
Because the first 17secs (!) sets the tone for your entire day ahead!
Then, throughout your day, you might want to come back and review your notes to remind yourself of the intention of the day, to help

YOU get back to the highest most shining version of YOU!

You are so, so loved.

I thank you from my heart for being here, for connecting, for CHOOSING the light in times that can seem darker when ever before if we don't choose our focus and train our minds carefully.
You are about to embark on a deeply transformative journey:
For the next 30days we will come together every morning and energetically we will be strongly connected throughout.
I want you to know I am 10000% here for you!

If you have any questions reach out to me privately on Instagram: @josephinemcgrail12

You are not alone. We are ALL ONE.

And now .. let's begin your Morning Rituals:

Step 1 Space:

Get comfy: choose a special place where you start YOUR day from every day for the next 30 days (today included). Sitting on your sofa/nice cushion in the corner/in your bed with your favourite scented candle on etc. Make it so inviting you would want to sit there all day- that kinda vibe.

Step 2 Breathe & Check In:

Close your eyes (NOT NOW OBVS). Place your hands on your heart. Breathe in deeply "I see you", exhale "I love you". Repeat for 2mins.

Pay close attention to ALL that may come up for you: all that your feeling, thinking and sensing just invite it all to flow through you.

Then start to ask yourself as you inhale: "how do I feel"? As you exhale allow the answer to land. Continue here for another 5 breaths. Stay open to how the answer may arrive: an image, a color, a feeling, a voice, a memory these are all valid and equally important for you today.

Now that you know a little bit more about how you are actually feeling at this moment in time move your hands down to your stomach: breathe in "what do I need?" Exhale allow that answer to land, continue here for another 5 breaths.

Step 3 High Vibes :

Now that you know whats really going on, what dialogue your mind is currently listening to we can take mindful actions to FINETUNE your current mood into one of LOVE, EXPANSION and CELEBRATION. WHAT you say? Bare with me:

Think of someone you LOVE unconditionally (BIG points if it's yourself). Remember the colour of their eyes, the warm smile they always give you, their scent, the last time you saw them. What did you do together? What time of day was it? What season? What were YOU wearing? How did it feel when they hugged YOU? Feel into that wonderful nourishing feeling of love starting at the heart spreading down all the way through to the toes and down through the arms and hands. Listen to their words now as they tell you how much YOU mean to them. How YOU are an inspiration in their life, how just knowing that YOU are apart of them makes them swell with love and pride.... THATS it beauty... NOW YOU GOT IT.... stay there. Close your eyes fall in love...stay there. Deep breath in, feeling all this love swirling around inside of you, when you are ready to exhale send ALL of your love right back to them thanking them for being in your life.

Step 4 Day Planning / Intention setting :

From this place of unconditional LOVE look at your day:

What simple steps can you make towards your dream today? Choose 3 things and write them here hehe yep YOU DECIDE which steps babe!! WHY YOU?!! Because YOU ARE THE ONLY ONE THAT KNOWS YOU! 123 GO:

1

2

3

Step 5 Inspiration:

Throughout today give yourself a few 5 mins breaks away from work either outdoors (double points again lol) or just closing your eyes hands on heart remembering your wonderful person you connected with this morning.

Tell yourself out loud "Im a fucking warrior mermaid princess and I'VE got this"

(repeat continually through out the day especially if doubt/ rational brain starts giving you all the reasons for why YOU CANT DO IT- in that case (shout it even louder)

Tell at least 1 person about your 30 Day Morning Miracle project. Accountability is one of our greatest cheerleaders so we like her:)

That's it. Now GO make this day YOURS.

Xxx Love Josephine

Day 2 Celebration

Good morning my love

Today is all about Celebrating YOU!!

So often in life we get so caught up with everything we feel we are not/don't have etc etc that we forget to CELEBRATE all that we already are, and have already achieved.
Today remind yourself that it is never the destination as such, but the JOURNEY that truly transforms us; the healing takes place when we are ready to receive, the teacher arrives when the student is open to learn. We simply start by starting.
So often we focus only on the end game and then, once we reach that, we are already on to the next....
Today I invite you to take the time to CELEBRATE your success of being the magnificent human being that you already are!
Give yourself permission to reward yourself NOW. Here. Today!
YOU as much as anyone else in the Universe deserves your love and affection!!
How will you celebrate YOU today? Perhaps by having a little more time to yourself today? Perhaps writing yourself a THANK YOU letter? Buy yourself flowers, enjoy a beautiful warm bath with essential oils, or simply by staying present today: whenever your mind goes into what you feel you are not, or don't have tell yourself:

'I am powerful and worthy. I am grateful for all that I am'.
I invite you to share how you are going to celebrate YOU today with

others: tell a friend or a colleague. Let's inspire each other to choose CELEBRATING all that we are and all that we are becoming!

Today I invite you to CELEBRATE yourself for committing to your dreams!! Yeah!!!

And on a side note: whenever we start prioritising our own dreams we have to sacrifice something else... whether that means less house work or less calling your poor old grandma, less eating all yummie cake or watching TV for hours... when we fully commit to our dreams something else gets sacrificed (at least for a little while;) But when we take something away/give something up, we need to add something instead!! That's where celebration comes in!!

You with me? Say: "YES I AM" LOUD NOW!!

Ok beauty, let's start your Morning Rituals:

Step 1 Space :

Go to your special place where you start YOUR day from. Sitting on your sofa/nice cushion in the corner/in your bed with your favourite scented candle on etc

Step 2 Breathe & Check In:

Close your eyes (NOT NOW OBVS). Place your hands on your heart. Breathe in deeply "I see you", exhale "I love you". Repeat for 2mins.

Pay close attention to ALL that may come up for you: all that your feeling, thinking and sensing just invite it all to flow through you.

Then start to ask yourself as you inhale: "how do I feel"? As you exhale allow the answer to land. Continue here for another 5 breaths. Stay open to how the answer may arrive: an image, a color, a feeling, a voice, a memory these are all valid and equally important for you today. Now that you know a little bit more about how you are actually feeling at this moment in time move your hands down to

your stomach: breathe in "what do I need?" Exhale allow that answer to land, continue here for another 5 breaths.

Step 3 High Vibes:

Now that you know whats really going on, what dialogue your mind is currently listening to we can take mindful actions to FINETUNE your current mood into one of LOVE, EXPANSION and CELEBRATION. WHAT you say? Bare with me:

Think of someone you LOVE unconditionally (BIG points if it's yourself). Remember the colour of their eyes, the warm smile they always give you, their scent, the last time you saw them. What did you do together? What time of day was it? What season? What were YOU wearing? How did it feel when they hugged YOU? That wonderful nourishing feeling of love starting at the heart spreading down all the way through to the toes and down through the arms and hands. Listen to their words now as they tell you how much YOU mean to them. How YOU are an inspiration in their life, how just knowing that YOU are apart of them makes them swell with love and pride.... THATS it beauty... NOW YOU GOT IT.... stay there. Close your eyes fall in love...stay there. Deep breath in, feeling all this love swirling around inside of you, when you are ready to exhale send ALL of your love right back to them thanking them for being in your life.

Step 4 Day Planning / Intention setting :

Now today I ask you to write down one thing you are going to do TODAY to CELEBRATE your success at rocking at achieving your dreams. Use your beautiful mind to create a perfect way for you to do this: perhaps stopping by your favourite cafe on the way home, going to a nice yoga/dance/acting class or any other hobbies you may have, watching a double episode on Netflix, have a long warm bath using essential oils and rose petals, buy yourself the most beautiful bouquet of flowers (and if YOU would easily do this TODAY buy the

BIGGEST or the one you would usually gladly buy a friend, but NOT yourself). Break down those old voices that are telling you that you are not worthy. YOU, my love could not be MORE DESERVING!!!

TODAY, I (your name:), promise to celebrate me and my success by :

1 (its a BIIIG one btw;)

2 (just in case you are like me and you LOOOOVE to celebrate)

3 (in case you are even more awesome and CAN'T wait to celebrate in many ways lol)

4(Ok babe thats enough for day 2!)

Step 5 Inspiration:

Remember we only ever do anything from a space of fear or love. Ask yourself throughout your day whether you are moving from a space of love or fear? What are you basing your decisions on? How are you communicating your truth?

Choose TODAY as your first day of living your life from a space of love and thus already now you can start by celebrating your wise decision to do so:)

Have a wonderful day by CREATING it that way!!!

xxxx Josephine

Day 3 Visualisation

Good morning beautiful,

Did I tell YOU how wonderful you are?

Did I tell you how proud I am of you: that you are committing to YOUR OWN HAPPINESS?

Yes I said that; YOU are the ONLY ONE that can ever make YOU truly happy!! Wtf?!!

No babe this is great news!! It means YOU are only ever responsible for YOUR OWN LIFE. You have the power to do this. For only YOU know what a happy life looks and feel like for YOU!!:)

AND RIGHT NOW, ON THIS GLORIOUS DAY, YOU ARE ON THE PATH OF SELFLOVE and SELFDISCOVERY ie on the EXPRESS train towards eternal JOY!!!:)

Just a gentle reminder to give yourself the gift of starting your Morning Miracle journey first thing - even before you are out of bed. Remember what I mentioned earlier? It is said that the first 17secs of being awake sets the tone for our entire day: ie whatever you think about during those precious first moments impacts how you feel, think and act throughout the rest of the day!! Imagine how your day would unfold if your first 17secs were filled with JOY, GRATITUDE and powerful INTENTIONS...? Imagine where that would take you...?

Now let's begin with our theme of today: Visualise to realise.
Since we were babies we have been practicing visualisation. We
mimicked our parents behaviour and we day dreamed about how we
ourselves would one day be adults, and have the power to create our
own life...
Only most of this visualisation was done unconsciously.
Which meant we, very likely, simply became more or less copies of
our parents including the good - and the not so good;)
Start TODAY, RIGHT NOW by consciously deciding how you want
to FEEL, ACT and THINK throughout your day today. Send love
ahead so that everyone you come into contact with will feel this
beautiful energy and reflect it back to you multiplied. Visualise
yourself throughout your day feeling Strong, Empowered, Rooted.
See yourself beaming with JOY and VITALITY and see yourself
leaving sparkles of beautiful energy behind you wherever you go
today.

"Remember the decisions we make today define our tomorrow"

Only YOU have the power to create your future self. And we start
right now!
Have a beautiful day by consciously visualising it so.
Love Josephine

Ok babe YOU'VE got this!! Now to work:

Step 1 Space :

Go to your special place where you start YOUR day. Sitting down
make yourself comfortable in the ways that you know best with your
favourite scented candle, incense, music or nothing but sacred
silence- up to you.

Step 2 Breathe & Check In:

Close your eyes (NOT NOW OBVS). Place your hands on your

heart. Breathe in deeply "I see you", exhale "I love you". Repeat for 2mins.

Pay close attention to ALL that may come up for you: all that your feeling, thinking and sensing just invite it all to flow through you.

Then start to ask yourself as you inhale: "how do I feel"? As you exhale allow the answer to land. Continue here for another 5 breaths. Stay open to how the answer may arrive: an image, a color, a feeling, a voice, a memory these are all valid and equally important for you today. Now that you know a little bit more about how you are actually feeling at this moment in time move your hands down to your stomach: breathe in "what do I need?" Exhale allow that answer to land, continue here for another 5 breaths.

Step 3 High Vibes :

Now that you know whats really going on, what dialogue your mind is currently listening to we can take mindful actions to FINETUNE your current mood into one of LOVE, EXPANSION and CELEBRATION. WHAT you say? Bare with me:

Think of someone you LOVE unconditionally (BIG points if it's yourself). Remember the colour of their eyes, the warm smile they always give you, their scent, the last time you saw them. What did you do together? What time of day was it? What season? What were YOU wearing? How did it feel when they hugged YOU? That wonderful nourishing feeling of love starting at the heart spreading down all the way through to the toes and down through the arms and hands. Listen to their words now as they tell you how much YOU mean to them. How YOU are an inspiration in their life, how just knowing that YOU are apart of them makes them swell with love and pride.... THATS it beauty... NOW YOU GOT IT.... stay there. Close your eyes fall in love...stay there. Deep breath in, feeling all this love swirling around inside of you, when you are ready to exhale send ALL of your love right back to them thanking them for being in your life.

Step 4 Day Planning / Intention setting :

From this place of unconditional LOVE look at your day:

What simple steps can you make towards your dream today? Choose 3 things and write them here hehe yep YOU DECIDE which steps babe!! WHY YOU?!! Because YOU ARE THE ONLY ONE THAT KNOWS YOU! 123 GO:

1

2

3

Thats it!!! How simple was that? And it took you like 10mins???Out of your entire day!!

Now one tiny little thing and then your off;)

(Promise)!!

Step 5 Inspiration:

I invite you to visualise YOUR IDEAL happy life and focus on how it makes you feel in the body. Do this with your eyes closed so your HEART and soul have space to speak.

Write down 3 things such as feelings, sensations and images that come up for you during this visualisation:

1

2

3

Day 4 Gratitude

Good morning my love and welcome to Day 4 which is all about Gratitude.

Take a moment after finishing your Morning Rituals to write down all that you FEEL (not think!) grateful for TODAY.
Everything that makes your heart sings and reminds YOU of just how ABUNDANT you already are.
When we CHOOSE to focus our full attention on ALL that is already good and magnificent about ourself and our life, we automatically heighten our energetic vibration and through that, we ensure MORE GOOD STUFF coming our way.

When we decide to change our focus from what we think is lacking to what is already opening/ wonderful/joyful we tell the Universe:
'This is what I LOVE' and the Universe lovingly return all of this, and more back to us, where ever we go:
even the most challenging times becomes lighter and brighter, we are met by supportive people who specialises in EXACTLY what we need at that time, we feel inspired and notices opportunities where ever we go etc.
Gratitude opens our hearts and melts away the doubt, fear and anger that have been keeping us small.
Gratitude sends us HOME to where we came from and where we truly belong:

Gratitude sends us HOME to our HEART.
Gratitude sends us HOME to ABUNDANCE and LOVE.
Have a beautiful day my love, by CHOOSING to focus on all that
YOU already ARE and all that you already HAVE.

Love Josephine

And now... it's time for your beautiful Morning Rituals of course!

Step 1 Space :

Go to your special place where you start YOUR day from. Enjoy
making yourself comfortable in the ways that you know best: with
your favourite scented candle etc.

Step 2 Breathe & Check In:

Close your eyes (NOT NOW OBVS). Place your hands on your
heart. Breathe in deeply "I see you", exhale "I love you". Repeat for
2mins.

Pay close attention to ALL that may come up for you: all that your
feeling, thinking and sensing just invite it all to flow through you.

Then start to ask yourself as you inhale: "how do I feel"? As you
exhale allow the answer to land. Continue here for another 5 breaths.
Stay open to how the answer may arrive: an image, a color, a feeling,
a voice, a memory these are all valid and equally important for you
today. Now that you know a little bit more about how you are
actually feeling at this moment in time, move your hands down to
your stomach: breathe in "what do I need?" Exhale, allow that
answer to land, continue here for another 5 breaths.

Step 3 High Vibes:

Now that you know what's really going on, what dialogue your mind
is currently listening to we can take mindful actions to FINETUNE
your current mood into one of LOVE, EXPANSION and
CELEBRATION. WHAT you say? Bare with me:

Think of someone you LOVE unconditionally (BIG points if it's yourself). Remember the colour of their eyes, the warm smile they always give you, their scent, the last time you saw them. What did you do together? What time of day was it? What season? What were YOU wearing? How did it feel when they hugged YOU? That wonderful nourishing feeling of love starting at the heart spreading down all the way through to the toes and down through the arms and hands. Listen to their words now as they tell you how much YOU mean to them. How YOU are an inspiration in their life, how just knowing that YOU are apart of them makes them swell with love and pride.... THATS it beauty... NOW YOU GOT IT.... stay there. Close your eyes fall in love...stay there. Deep breath in, feeling all this love swirling around inside of you, when you are ready to exhale send ALL of your love right back to them thanking them for being in your life.

Step 4 Day Planning / Intention setting :

From this place of unconditional LOVE look at your day:

What simple steps can you make towards your dream today? Choose 3 things and write them here hehe yep YOU DECIDE which steps babe!! WHY YOU?!! Because YOU ARE THE ONLY ONE THAT KNOWS YOU! 123 GO:

1

2

3

Step 5 Inspiration:

Write down at least 3 things which are ALREADY good in your life right now!

1

2

Day 5 Trust & allow time to blossom

Welcome to this new day beautiful soul,

Take a moment to recognize the gift it is to wake up healthy and alive. To feel the sunlight on your skin and to hear the birds sing.

Today I will open up with a simple and yet super powerful saying; " The last thing to flower on a fruit tree is the fruit"!
Take a moment to make yourself comfortable as you take a nice deep breathe in welcoming in this BRAND new day. What beautiful experiences will today bring?
So often in life we wish we could control and determine the outcomes, and not being able to can really throw us off cause.
However my love, as always when we return to nature, we see time and time again that EVERYTHING that was created by the Universe has it's own perfect and miraculous rhythms:
A tree knows when it is time to release its seedlings... when it is time to shed its leaves... when it is time to go within and draw its energy in and down to protect itself during the cold winter months.
It doesn't DOUBT or QUESTION the rhythm of Nature.
It simply TRUSTS.
This doesn't mean that it doesn't take action (in fact for a 'still grounded' being trees are surprisingly busy with all sorts of things- they live in family systems and protect each other and communicates if danger or illness arrises).
However they don't worry about whether or not it will ever be Spring

again! They 100% TRUST in Life. And through trusting they themselves are FREE to enjoy each and every moment as the gift it is.

Today my loves let's decide to TRUST! In yourself, in the process, in life, in the Universe.

Allow time to do its magical healing work.

Whatever has happened it's in the past, and its time to move forward understanding that our past only ever has power over us if we decide to LET IT.

The final thing to blossom on a fruit tree are the fruits!

Connect with that part of you that TRUSTS today and go out there and be inspired by the trees.

Love you xxx Josephine

Ps. Remember the tree doesn't stop trusting in Nature or the Universe just because it's fruits may not appear as fast or in the quantities that the tree may like... The tree simply trust. It keeps doing its thing in a relaxed and easy manner: this deep, intuitive inner knowing allows it to go about its everyday business without stressing out over when the fruits themselves may or may not arrive.

The tree knows that life is always there watching, supporting and loving it. And through that trust the tree gracefully goes on being a tree without a worry in the world.

(other things may upset the tree temporarily such as a newly planted foreign plant that might be poisonous to its family root system etc however then the tree will take action there and then and then afterwards... you know it: go on being a tree)

Today TRUST LIKE A TREE! And now let's begin your Morning Rituals:

Step 1 Space :

Go to your special place where you start YOUR day. Sitting down make yourself comfortable in the ways that you know best with your favourite scented candle, incense, music or nothing but sacred silence- up to you.

Step 2 Breathe & Check In:

Close your eyes (NOT NOW OBVS). Place your hands on your heart. Breathe in deeply "I see you", exhale "I love you". Repeat for 2mins.

Pay close attention to ALL that may come up for you: all that your feeling, thinking and sensing just invite it all to flow through you.

Then start to ask yourself as you inhale: "how do I feel"? As you exhale allow the answer to land. Continue here for another 5 breaths. Stay open to how the answer may arrive: an image, a color, a feeling, a voice, a memory these are all valid and equally important for you today. Now that you know a little bit more about how you are actually feeling at this moment in time move your hands down to your stomach: breathe in "what do I need?" Exhale allow that answer to land, continue here for another 5 breaths.

Step 3 High Vibes :

Now that you know whats really going on, what dialogue your mind is currently listening to we can take mindful actions to FINETUNE your current mood into one of LOVE, EXPANSION and CELEBRATION. WHAT you say? Bare with me: Think of someone you LOVE unconditionally (BIG points if it's yourself). Remember the colour of their eyes, the warm smile they always give you, their scent, the last time you saw them. What did you do together? What time of day was it? What season? What were YOU wearing? How did it feel when they hugged YOU? That wonderful nourishing feeling of love starting at the heart spreading down all the way through to the toes and down through the arms and hands. Listen to their words now as they tell you how much YOU mean to them. How YOU are an inspiration in their life, how just knowing that YOU are apart of them makes them swell with love and pride.... THATS it beauty... NOW YOU GOT IT.... stay there. Close your eyes fall in love...stay there. Deep breath in, feeling all this love swirling around inside of you, when you are ready to exhale send ALL of your love right back to them thanking them for being in your life.

Step 4 Day Planning / Intention setting :

From this place of unconditional LOVE look at your day:

What simple steps can you make towards your dream today? Choose 3 things and write them here hehe yep YOU DECIDE which steps babe!! WHY YOU?!! Because YOU ARE THE ONLY ONE THAT KNOWS YOU! 123 GO:

1

2

3

Thats it!!! How simple was that? And it took you like 10mins???Out of your entire day!!

Now one tiny little thing and then your off;)

(Promise)!!

Step 5 Inspiration:

I invite you to think about 10 ways to help you TRUST more in yourself, in others and in LIFE. What could you do to help yourself find that deep trust within your heart? Perhaps start keeping a gratitude journal where you each night write down what made you feel save and loved that day? Perhaps challenge your limited beliefs systems ie challenge your fears? Perhaps start coaching sessions (call me!!;) You got this babe!!

1

2

3

4

5

6

7

8

9

10

Day 6 Look For Miracles

Whoop whoop YOU are SO amazing!! Now already on day 6 and you know what? It is starting to SHOW!! In the way your eyes shine, the glow of your skin and the awesome GOOD VIBES you are sending out everywhere you go!!

THIS my love means you are well on your way!! And the fantastic news is that this will continue more and more everyday! As YOU make the commitment to continue YOUR TRUTH you will every day get a HUGE BOOST of CONFIDENCE:) A massive FUCK IM AMAZING kinda boost!!! Yeah!!!

Repeat after me: "I FINALLY KNOW MY WORTH AND I AM READY TO SHINE!! TODAY IS MY DAY!!"

Yeah babe!!! Let's get ready for this brand new day by enjoying your Morning Rituals:

Step 1 Space :

Go to your special place where you start YOUR day. Sitting down make yourself comfortable in the ways that you know best with your favourite scented candle, incense, music or nothing but sacred silence- up to you.

Step 2 Breathe & Check In:

Close your eyes (NOT NOW OBVS). Place your hands on your heart. Breathe in deeply "I see you", exhale "I love you". Repeat for 2mins.

Pay close attention to ALL that may come up for you: all that your feeling, thinking and sensing just invite it all to flow through you.

Then start to ask yourself as you inhale: "how do I feel"? As you exhale allow the answer to land. Continue here for another 5 breaths. Stay open to how the answer may arrive: an image, a color, a feeling, a voice, a memory these are all valid and equally important for you today. Now that you know a little bit more about how you are actually feeling at this moment in time move your hands down to your stomach: breathe in "what do I need?" Exhale allow that answer to land, continue here for another 5 breaths.

Step 3 High Vibes :

Now that you know whats really going on, what dialogue your mind is currently listening to we can take mindful actions to FINETUNE your current mood into one of LOVE, EXPANSION and CELEBRATION. WHAT you say? Bare with me:

Think of someone you LOVE unconditionally (BIG points if it's yourself). Remember the colour of their eyes, the warm smile they always give you, their scent, the last time you saw them. What did you do together? What time of day was it? What season? What were YOU wearing? How did it feel when they hugged YOU? That wonderful nourishing feeling of love starting at the heart spreading down all the way through to the toes and down through the arms and hands. Listen to their words now as they tell you how much YOU mean to them. How YOU are an inspiration in their life, how just knowing that YOU are apart of them makes them swell with love and pride.... THATS it beauty... NOW YOU GOT IT.... stay there. Close your eyes fall in love...stay there. Deep breath in, feeling all this love swirling around inside of you, when you are ready to exhale send

ALL of your love right back to them thanking them for being in your life.

Step 4 Day Planning/ Intention Settting:

Make it your intention to look for miracles; Big and small!! Miracles are literally ANYTHING at all that reconfirms back to you that you are f*king amazing by making you feel awesome!!

Step 5 Inspiration:

TONIGHT write down 3 miracles that happened today ie: your bus arrived exactly when you needed it, a good friend called you as you were thinking of them. The shop had the dress you wanted in the size you needed, the sun rose! The sun set! (yes those two are BIG miracles that most of us take for granted) YOU woke up ALIVE and WELL! The entrance at work had been renovated, they had flowers at work now. Etc etc

START LOOKING AROUND:

1

2

3

4 Yeah babe I know YOU saw more than 3 lol

5 Extra brownie points for you:)

Day 7 Reflections

Good morning beautiful you and welcome to day 7.
It has been one week now!!
For one week YOU have decided to stay TRUE to YOU, to your intention, to your WHY:)
I am SO SOOOO proud of you!

If you know you can do 7days you know you can do another!!- It'a one of those milestones that somehow makes us realize that we have MOVED beyond... that we have transcended a part of our old (and UNTRUE) believe systems of what we can and cannot do!! The new words are now:

"I am a winner and YES I CAN do it"

I love you babe. Not much talk today; just KEEP DOING WHAT YOUR DOING-

It's working WONDERS!!

And- honestly this makes me so happy as I KNOW that if you can do a week you can do even more ie YOU ARE READY TO GO EVEN DEEPER INTO YOUR JOURNEY OF TRANSFORMATION!!
So often in life we stop just when it is about to get interesting.... a new relationship... a new hobby... a new diet... manifesting our dreams..?;)!!!

CONGRATULATE yourself for your commitment to your highest wellness of mind body and soul.

For saying YES I AM READY!!!

Ready for LOVE
Ready to be LOVED
Ready to LOVE
Ready to TRUST
Ready to RELEASE
Ready to FORGIVE
Ready to SHINE MY LIGHT
Ready to LIVE MY PURPOSE
Ready to OPEN
Ready to TAKE CHARGE
Ready to RISE

We are ready to rise.

Have a beautiful day- you have done amazing!!!

Love you xxxx Josephine

Step 1 Space :

Go to your special place where you start YOUR day. Sitting down make yourself comfortable in the ways that you know best with your favourite scented candle, incense, music or nothing but sacred silence- up to you.

Step 2 Breathe & Check In:

Close your eyes (NOT NOW OBVS). Place your hands on your heart. Breathe in deeply "I see you", exhale "I love you". Repeat for 2mins.

Pay close attention to ALL that may come up for you: all that your feeling, thinking and sensing just invite it all to flow through you.

Then start to ask yourself as you inhale: "how do I feel"? As you exhale allow the answer to land. Continue here for another 5 breaths. Stay open to how the answer may arrive: an image, a color, a feeling, a voice, a memory these are all valid and equally important for you today. Now that you know a little bit more about how you are actually feeling at this moment in time move your hands down to your stomach: breathe in "what do I need?" Exhale allow that answer to land, continue here for another 5 breaths.

Step 3 High Vibes :

Now that you know whats really going on, what dialogue your mind is currently listening to we can take mindful actions to FINETUNE your current mood into one of LOVE, EXPANSION and CELEBRATION. WHAT you say? Bare with me:

Think of someone you LOVE unconditionally (BIG points if it's yourself). Remember the colour of their eyes, the warm smile they always give you, their scent, the last time you saw them. What did you do together? What time of day was it? What season? What were YOU wearing? How did it feel when they hugged YOU? That wonderful nourishing feeling of love starting at the heart spreading down all the way through to the toes and down through the arms and hands. Listen to their words now as they tell you how much YOU mean to them. How YOU are an inspiration in their life, how just knowing that YOU are apart of them makes them swell with love and pride.... THATS it beauty... NOW YOU GOT IT.... stay there. Close your eyes fall in love...stay there. Deep breath in, feeling all this love swirling around inside of you, when you are ready to exhale send ALL of your love right back to them thanking them for being in your life.

Step 4 Day Planning / Intention setting :

From this place of unconditional LOVE look at your day:

What simple steps can you make towards your dream today? Choose 3 things and write them here hehe yep YOU DECIDE which steps babe!! WHY YOU?!! Because YOU ARE THE ONLY ONE THAT KNOWS YOU! 123 GO:

1

2

3

Step 5 Inspiration:

Take a moment to reflect back on the past week. How have you been feeling? What changes have you started to implement (including doing The 30 Day Morning Miracle)? Write down 5 things that have already transformed and is continueing to change in your life RIGHT NOW. Think about all areas of your life (from how you feel mentally, emotionally, physically and even spiritually) remembering that we are multi dimensional beings having a human experience. My new life, this NEW ME is now:

1

2

3

4

5

Day 8 Inspiration

Morning gorgeous!!

Do you know how LOVED you are?!!!

Today is all about YOU staying, feeling and being INSPIRED to grow and expand even further!! Many stop simply because they LOOSE their inspiration ie the motivation of WHY they started in the first place! So my love, WHATEVER it is YOU decided 8 days ago, and which is currently YOUR goal/dream/focus, use today to find inspiration to keep you focused and HYPED to take it even further!

When you reach step 5 this morning spend 5mins to research some inspirational people whom YOU feel truly inspire you. Whatever their qualities, the MAIN thing is that YOU feel elevated and encouraged to move onwards and up simply by thinking about them!!!

Today, consciously, more than ever before, let yourself be UPLIFTED and MOTIVATED by choosing WHO, WHAT and WHERE truly inspires you.

Everything is energy, including us! So choosing wisely whom you share your energy with will literally impact ALL levels of your existence.

YOU ARE LOVE

xxxx Josephine

Now let's begin, it's time for your Morning Rituals

Step 1 Space :

Go to your special place where you start YOUR day. Sitting down make yourself comfortable in the ways that you know best with your favourite scented candle, incense, music or nothing but sacred silence- up to you.

Step 2 Breathe & Check In:

Close your eyes (NOT NOW OBVS). Place your hands on your heart. Breathe in deeply "I see you", exhale "I love you". Repeat for 2mins.

Pay close attention to ALL that may come up for you: all that your feeling, thinking and sensing just invite it all to flow through you.

Then start to ask yourself as you inhale: "how do I feel"? As you exhale allow the answer to land. Continue here for another 5 breaths. Stay open to how the answer may arrive: an image, a color, a feeling, a voice, a memory these are all valid and equally important for you today. Now that you know a little bit more about how you are actually feeling at this moment in time move your hands down to your stomach: breathe in "what do I need?" Exhale allow that answer to land, continue here for another 5 breaths.

Step 3 High Vibes :

Now that you know whats really going on, what dialogue your mind is currently listening to we can take mindful actions to FINETUNE your current mood into one of LOVE, EXPANSION and CELEBRATION. WHAT you say? Bare with me:

Think of someone you LOVE unconditionally (BIG points if it's yourself). Remember the colour of their eyes, the warm smile they always give you, their scent, the last time you saw them. What did

you do together? What time of day was it? What season? What were YOU wearing? How did it feel when they hugged YOU? That wonderful nourishing feeling of love starting at the heart spreading down all the way through to the toes and down through the arms and hands. Listen to their words now as they tell you how much YOU mean to them. How YOU are an inspiration in their life, how just knowing that YOU are apart of them makes them swell with love and pride.... THATS it beauty... NOW YOU GOT IT.... stay there. Close your eyes fall in love...stay there. Deep breath in, feeling all this love swirling around inside of you, when you are ready to exhale send ALL of your love right back to them thanking them for being in your life.

Step 4 Day Planning / Intention setting :

From this place of unconditional LOVE look at your day:

What simple steps can you make towards your dream today? Choose 3 things and write them here hehe yep YOU DECIDE which steps babe!! WHY YOU?!! Because YOU ARE THE ONLY ONE THAT KNOWS YOU! 123 GO:

1

2

3

Step 5 Inspiration:

Spend 5 minutes now researching/remembering who truly inspires you? Can be from all walks of life, near or far, passed over or still alive including saints, angels, spirit animals, elementals, star people etc etc anything and everything- whatever makes YOU feel inspired and motivated to be your greatest most divine version of YOU:) Write them all down here and continue on in your journal if you run out of space;)

Day 9 Letting go of the bullshit

Morning gorgeous!!

Did you wake up with that F* I can't do it!??

TODAY I just want one day to myself where I don't have to do the hard work ie putting in the effort to achieve my dreams????

Guess what that means that RIGHT NOW YOU are standing on the edge of a cliff wanting SO badly to jump but feeling concerned you may have forgotten how to fly?;)!!!

It is TODAY, in this very moment, that YOU have the opportunity to claim back your power and through the jumping realise that YOU HAVE ALWAYS known how to fly!!!

It is by CHOOSING TO LET Go Of The Bullshit that we transcend and rise above our old limited beliefs that have KEPT US FROM LIVING OUR AUTHENTIC DREAMLIFE.

So today my love, more than ever before don't just walk to the edge and hang out there; choose to RUN TO and then JUMP OFF THE CLIFF whilst SHOUTING from the top of your lungs : " I CHOOSE ME! I AM MY OWN GREATEST CHEERLEADER and I AM GOING TO MAKE IT"

You ready babe?;)!!!

GO GET THEM!!!

Love xxx Josephine

Time for your Morning Rituals YEAH:

Step 1 Space :

Go to your special place where you start YOUR day. Sitting down make yourself comfortable in the ways that you know best with your favourite scented candle, incense, music or nothing but sacred silence- up to you.

Step 2 Breathe & Check In:

Close your eyes (NOT NOW OBVS). Place your hands on your heart. Breathe in deeply "I see you", exhale "I love you". Repeat for 2mins.

Pay close attention to ALL that may come up for you: all that your feeling, thinking and sensing just invite it all to flow through you.

Then start to ask yourself as you inhale: "how do I feel"? As you exhale allow the answer to land. Continue here for another 5 breaths. Stay open to how the answer may arrive: an image, a color, a feeling, a voice, a memory these are all valid and equally important for you today. Now that you know a little bit more about how you are actually feeling at this moment in time move your hands down to your stomach: breathe in "what do I need?" Exhale allow that answer to land, continue here for another 5 breaths.

Step 3 High Vibes :

Now that you know whats really going on, what dialogue your mind is currently listening to we can take mindful actions to FINETUNE your current mood into one of LOVE, EXPANSION and CELEBRATION. WHAT you say? Bare with me:

Think of someone you LOVE unconditionally (BIG points if it's yourself). Remember the colour of their eyes, the warm smile they always give you, their scent, the last time you saw them. What did

you do together? What time of day was it? What season? What were YOU wearing? How did it feel when they hugged YOU? That wonderful nourishing feeling of love starting at the heart spreading down all the way through to the toes and down through the arms and hands. Listen to their words now as they tell you how much YOU mean to them. How YOU are an inspiration in their life, how just knowing that YOU are apart of them makes them swell with love and pride.... THATS it beauty... NOW YOU GOT IT.... stay there. Close your eyes fall in love...stay there. Deep breath in, feeling all this love swirling around inside of you, when you are ready to exhale send ALL of your love right back to them thanking them for being in your life.

Step 4 Day Planning / Intention setting :

From this place of unconditional LOVE look at your day:

What simple steps can you make towards your dream today? Choose 3 things and write them here hehe yep YOU DECIDE which steps babe!! WHY YOU?!! Because YOU ARE THE ONLY ONE THAT KNOWS YOU! 123 GO:

1

2

3

That's it!!! How simple was that? And it took you like 10mins???Out of your entire day!!

Now one tiny little thing and then your off;)

(Promise)!!

Step 5 Inspiration:

Ask yourself: "where in my life am I ready to let go"?
"Who/what/why am I ready to release"? "What would happen if I let
it go"? "How would these changes positively impact myself and my
loved ones"?

Write down your thoughts and answers here:

Day 10 Share your success

Helloooo yeah your back! You woke up alive and healthy and are now taking this time for YOU to ensure you make the most of this beautiful day!!

Today I invite you to share 3 stories of success with whomever you choose!

Make them as vivid as possible talk in colours and feelings and notice how it makes YOU feel to share your own beautiful inspiring stories of success.

Choose them now:

1

2

3

And remember SUCCESS can be absolutely ANYTHING you did, decided on, thought, took action on!! The ONLY thing that can ever make anything a success is measured on how it makes you FEEL!! So babe ANYTHING YOU created that made you FEEL amazing is an incredible SUCCESS!!

Just like how you RIGHT NOW IN THIS VERY MOMENT got out of bed early to make time for your 30 Day Morning Miracle transformation..;)!! You get me?

Love you, xx Josephine

YEAH let's start your Morning Rituals

Step 1 Space :

Go to your special place where you start YOUR day. Sitting down make yourself comfortable in the ways that you know best with your favourite scented candle, incense, music or nothing but sacred silence- up to you.

Step 2 Breathe & Check In:

Close your eyes (NOT NOW OBVS). Place your hands on your heart. Breathe in deeply "I see you", exhale "I love you". Repeat for 2mins.

Pay close attention to ALL that may come up for you: all that your feeling, thinking and sensing just invite it all to flow through you.

Then start to ask yourself as you inhale: "how do I feel"? As you exhale allow the answer to land. Continue here for another 5 breaths. Stay open to how the answer may arrive: an image, a color, a feeling, a voice, a memory these are all valid and equally important for you today. Now that you know a little bit more about how you are actually feeling at this moment in time move your hands down to your stomach: breathe in "what do I need?" Exhale allow that answer to land, continue here for another 5 breaths.

Step 3 High Vibes :

Now that you know whats really going on, what dialogue your mind is currently listening to we can take mindful actions to FINETUNE your current mood into one of LOVE, EXPANSION and CELEBRATION. WHAT you say? Bare with me:

Think of someone you LOVE unconditionally (BIG points if it's yourself). Remember the colour of their eyes, the warm smile they always give you, their scent, the last time you saw them. What did

you do together? What time of day was it? What season? What were YOU wearing? How did it feel when they hugged YOU? That wonderful nourishing feeling of love starting at the heart spreading down all the way through to the toes and down through the arms and hands. Listen to their words now as they tell you how much YOU mean to them. How YOU are an inspiration in their life, how just knowing that YOU are apart of them makes them swell with love and pride.... THATS it beauty... NOW YOU GOT IT.... stay there. Close your eyes fall in love...stay there. Deep breath in, feeling all this love swirling around inside of you, when you are ready to exhale send ALL of your love right back to them thanking them for being in your life.

Step 4 Day Planning / Intention setting :

From this place of unconditional LOVE look at your day:

What simple steps can you make towards your dream today? Choose 3 things and write them here hehe yep YOU DECIDE which steps babe!! WHY YOU?!! Because YOU ARE THE ONLY ONE THAT KNOWS YOU! 123 GO:

1

2

3

Step 5 Inspiration:

Have a think about what success means to you. Who in your life do you see as being successful? Remember, the ONLY true success there ever exists is what YOU give value to. Challenge how you see success by asking yourself "does this really matter to me? Will doing this/having/being that truly bring me happiness"? "Who gave me those beliefs"? "What would happen if I created my own version of success"?

Finally ask yourself " ISN'T THE HIGHEST VERSION OF LIVING A SUCCESSFUL LIFE SIMPLY TO BE HAPPY? AND AS I AM THE ONLY ONE WHO TRULY KNOWS WHAT MAKES ME HAPPY I MUST ALSO BE THE ONLY ONE WHO KNOWS WHAT SUCCESS LOOKS AND FEELS LIKE TO ME"?

Now write down your own version of success here:

Day 11 Step by step COMMITMENT

Morning beautiful. SO today is all about recognizing that everything takes time to build. Instead of doing it ALL today (which by the way just isn't possible even if you wanted to) the way to succeed in ANY area of your life is to do a little EVERY. SINGLE. DAY.

It's through feeding your dreams with your beautiful attention in a way that feels uplifting and joyful:)

Whether that means going to the library to research, to an exhibition or a workshop, buying a few essentials that will make it easier and more achievable for you to materialise your dream. You name it. Be adventurous!! The key is this: ANYTHING you want to grow YOU have to take action. Little or big. BUT do it every single day.

Today write down 3 simple actions you are COMMITED to take TODAY to help create your dream life:

1

2

3

And yes, we still have to go through step 1-4 as well now. WHY? Because it creates DISCIPLINE which is EXACTLY what we need to carry us through on the days when motivation doesn't feel strong lol. And trust me babe we ALL have days like that!! I hear you!! However the ONLY thing that sets YOU aside from the majority is your COMMITMENT to living YOUR MOST INCREDIBLE DREAMLIFE. Step by step, day by day WE keep on going!! Always expanding and FOREVER GROWING:) HELL YEAH BABE: TODAY IS YOUR DAY!!!! LET'S RISE!

Seduce your dream into manifesting by treating your dream like a beautiful lover: dress up, put on your best outfit and take charge! Your dreams deserve the best most brightest version of YOU. So my love, ask yourself " Who will I be today"? "How will I show up today"?

Love xxx Josephine

Time for showing up to your Morning Miracles:

Step 1 Space :

Go to your special place where you start YOUR day. Sitting down make yourself comfortable in the ways that you know best with your favourite scented candle, incense, music or nothing but sacred silence- up to you.

Step 2 Breathe & Check In:

Close your eyes (NOT NOW OBVS). Place your hands on your heart. Breathe in deeply "I see you", exhale "I love you". Repeat for 2mins.

Pay close attention to ALL that may come up for you: all that your feeling, thinking and sensing just invite it all to flow through you.

Then start to ask yourself as you inhale: "how do I feel"? As you exhale allow the answer to land. Continue here for another 5 breaths. Stay open to how the answer may arrive: an image, a colour, a feeling, a voice, a memory these are all valid and equally important for you today. Now that you know a little bit more about how you are actually feeling at this moment in time move your hands down to your stomach: breathe in "what do I need?" Exhale allow that answer to land, continue here for another 5 breaths.

Step 3 High Vibes :

Now that you know whats really going on, what dialogue your mind is currently listening to we can take mindful actions to FINETUNE your current mood into one of LOVE, EXPANSION and CELEBRATION. WHAT you say? Bare with me:

Think of someone you LOVE unconditionally (BIG points if it's yourself). Remember the colour of their eyes, the warm smile they always give you, their scent, the last time you saw them. What did you do together? What time of day was it? What season? What were YOU wearing? How did it feel when they hugged YOU? That wonderful nourishing feeling of love starting at the heart spreading down all the way through to the toes and down through the arms and hands. Listen to their words now as they tell you how much YOU mean to them. How YOU are an inspiration in their life, how just knowing that YOU are apart of them makes them swell with love and pride.... THATS it beauty... NOW YOU GOT IT.... stay there. Close your eyes fall in love...stay there. Deep breath in, feeling all this love swirling around inside of you, when you are ready to exhale send ALL of your love right back to them thanking them for being in your life.

Step 4 Day Planning / Intention setting :

From this place of unconditional LOVE look at your day:

What simple steps can you make towards your dream today? Choose 3 things and write them here hehe yep YOU DECIDE which steps babe!! WHY YOU?!! Because YOU ARE THE ONLY ONE THAT KNOWS YOU! 123 GO:

1

2

Thats it!!! How simple was that? And it took you like 10mins???Out of your entire day!!

Now one tiny little thing and then your off;)

(Promise)!!

Step 5 Inspiration:

Everything and everyone started somewhere! Whoever you feel inspired by once sat like you feeling overwhelmed and scared... Any book, movie, song anything that was ever created started somewhere out of no more than an idea.. an instinct...a hint..

The only thing that stands between you and whomever you look up to is that they started! Just like YOU are right now on your journey of transformation. Just like YOU every day commit to getting up earlier in time for your Morning Rituals.

EVERYTHING & EVERYONE STARTS BY STARTING. Simple!

Day 12 The power of the present

Good morning gorgeous, great to see you are here again!!

Today we will focus on being present. Being RIGHT HERE, RIGHT NOW. Sounds easy? Hmmm.. all though your body is very much here your mind, your awareness, is usually still chewing on something that took place in the past or might happen in the future. It is sad to say, but the truth is most of the time we are simply not here. That means we are MISSING out on life!!

So what do we do about it?

The easiest way to change this is by becoming aware of your senses. Try it right now:

Listen to the sounds that are far away... hear them... ok now focus on the ones that are closer by... then finally rest on the sound of your own breathe, feel your own heart beating.

Just feel into your heart, you can place your hands there now if that feels right. Just FEEL into your heart. How strong is that beat? What feelings arise when you breathe deeper? Inhale for 12345 hold it, exhale for 54321 hold it. Repeat these deep breathes a couple more times.

As you go about your day make it your top priority to really SEE, SMELL, HEAR, FEEL and TASTE life. When you are with people focus all of your attention on the sound of their voice, the feeling about them and the smells around them..

As you walk down the street try aand feel your feet touching the ground, notice how the Earth holds and supports you. Notice the temperatures around you. Pay FULL attention to how your body ie your senses are responding to each moment. And whenever you see your mind wandering off into the past or into the future ie away from RIGHT NOW come back to your senses; what can you hear? What can you smell etc etc. This is one of my most powerful tools to living a healthy radiant life. And now it can be yours too:) Have a beautiful day my love- stay PRESENT. Be a gift to your surroundings.

xxx Josephine

Now let's enjoy your Morning Rituals:

Step 1 Space :

Go to your special place where you start YOUR day. Sitting down make yourself comfortable in the ways that you know best with your favourite scented candle, incense, music or nothing but sacred silence- up to you.

Step 2 Breathe & Check In:

Close your eyes (NOT NOW OBVS). Place your hands on your heart. Breathe in deeply "I see you", exhale "I love you". Repeat for 2mins.

Pay close attention to ALL that may come up for you: all that your feeling, thinking and sensing just invite it all to flow through you.

Then start to ask yourself as you inhale: "how do I feel"? As you exhale allow the answer to land. Continue here for another 5 breaths. Stay open to how the answer may arrive: an image, a colour, a feeling, a voice, a memory these are all valid and equally important for you today. Now that you know a little bit more about how you are actually feeling at this moment in time move your hands down to

your stomach: breathe in "what do I need?" Exhale allow that answer to land, continue here for another 5 breaths.

Step 3 High Vibes :

Now that you know whats really going on, what dialogue your mind is currently listening to we can take mindful actions to FINETUNE your current mood into one of LOVE, EXPANSION and CELEBRATION. WHAT you say? Bare with me:

Think of someone you LOVE unconditionally (BIG points if it's yourself). Remember the colour of their eyes, the warm smile they always give you, their scent, the last time you saw them. What did you do together? What time of day was it? What season? What were YOU wearing? How did it feel when they hugged YOU? That wonderful nourishing feeling of love starting at the heart spreading down all the way through to the toes and down through the arms and hands. Listen to their words now as they tell you how much YOU mean to them. How YOU are an inspiration in their life, how just knowing that YOU are apart of them makes them swell with love and pride.... THATS it beauty... NOW YOU GOT IT.... stay there. Close your eyes fall in love...stay there. Deep breath in, feeling all this love swirling around inside of you, when you are ready to exhale send ALL of your love right back to them thanking them for being in your life.

Step 4 Day Planning / Intention setting :

From this place of unconditional LOVE look at your day:

What simple steps can you make towards your dream today? Choose 3 things and write them here hehe yep YOU DECIDE which steps babe!! WHY YOU?!! Because YOU ARE THE ONLY ONE THAT KNOWS YOU! 123 GO:

1

2

3

Thats it!!! How simple was that? And it took you like 10mins???Out of your entire day!!

Now one tiny little thing and then your off;)

(Promise)!!

Step 5 Inspiration:

The only moment that is every truly ours is the here and now. RIGHT NOW as you are reading these lines notice the sounds around you, the feeling in your body, the breath in your lungs. What RIGHT HERE, RIGHT NOW is already good in your life? Write this down now:

1

2

3

4 (and continue in your journal if you like)

Day 13 Your words have power

Your words are your prayers. Today pay close attention to how you speak about yourself and to yourself. Which thoughts do you pay attention to? Try it now: put your timer to 1 min and write down the majority of the words you hear in your mind. Have a look at them and decide whether these are serving you or not? If not write down their opposites: if you wrote failure change it to success, tired to rejuvenated etc etc. Now watch which words you are choosing as you go about your day ie how you speak about yourself – your dreams your aspirations, your work, your physical appearance, your mind etc etc these all make up YOU.

Everything starts in the mind and from there our entire life is created so TODAY is where the real work starts my love. I know YOU are ready for this challenge, that YOU are ready to take yourself to the next level of conscious awareness.

Choose ONLY thoughts and words that uplifts and inspires you.

It may feel like you are brain washing yourself at first but stick with it my love and I promise you are going to see and feel the results. As you change your thoughts and your words you change your entire life experience: "as you change your thoughts about the world the world itself changes".

Love Josephine

With this in mind let's start your beautiful, uplifting Morning Rituals:

Step 1 Space :

Go to your special place where you start YOUR day. Sitting down make yourself comfortable in the ways that you know best with your favourite scented candle, incense, music or nothing but sacred silence- up to you.

Step 2 Breathe & Check In:

Close your eyes (NOT NOW OBVS). Place your hands on your heart. Breathe in deeply "I see you", exhale "I love you". Repeat for 2mins.

Pay close attention to ALL that may come up for you: all that your feeling, thinking and sensing just invite it all to flow through you.

Then start to ask yourself as you inhale: "how do I feel"? As you exhale allow the answer to land. Continue here for another 5 breaths. Stay open to how the answer may arrive: an image, a color, a feeling, a voice, a memory these are all valid and equally important for you today. Now that you know a little bit more about how you are actually feeling at this moment in time move your hands down to your stomach: breathe in "what do I need?" Exhale allow that answer to land, continue here for another 5 breaths.

Step 3 High Vibes :

Now that you know whats really going on, what dialogue your mind is currently listening to we can take mindful actions to FINETUNE your current mood into one of LOVE, EXPANSION and CELEBRATION. WHAT you say? Bare with me:

Think of someone you LOVE unconditionally (BIG points if it's yourself). Remember the colour of their eyes, the warm smile they always give you, their scent, the last time you saw them. What did you do together? What time of day was it? What season? What were YOU wearing? How did it feel when they hugged YOU? That wonderful nourishing feeling of love starting at the heart spreading down all the way through to the toes and down through the arms and hands. Listen to their words now as they tell you how much YOU mean to them. How YOU are an inspiration in their life, how just knowing that YOU are apart of them makes them swell with love and pride.... THATS it beauty... NOW YOU GOT IT.... stay there. Close your eyes fall in love...stay there. Deep breath in, feeling all this love swirling around inside of you, when you are ready to exhale send ALL of your love right back to them thanking them for being in your life.

Step 4 Day Planning / Intention setting :

From this place of unconditional LOVE look at your day:

What simple steps can you make towards your dream today? Choose 3 things and write them here hehe yep YOU DECIDE which steps babe!! WHY YOU?!! Because YOU ARE THE ONLY ONE THAT KNOWS YOU! 123 GO:

1

2

3

Thats it!!! How simple was that? And it took you like 10mins???Out of your entire day!!

Now one tiny little thing and then your off;)

(Promise)!!

Step 5 Inspiration:

What words do you use most frequently? Set a timer for 1minute and write them down now:

1

2

3

4

5

6

7

8

etc

Then look back and see if they are truly serving you? And if not
DECIDE to only use words that empower you and make you feel
amazing!!! Write these down now:

1

2

3

4

5

6

7

etc

Day 14 You are already loved

Everything we do in life is based on choices we make either from a space of fear or love. Ask yourself RIGHT NOW: what am I basing my choices on?

Really listen... If you took fear out of the equation how would that change your decisions? What would you do TODAY if you knew you couldn't fail? Once we understand that everything we ever do in life is because we think we will either be happier or at least less scared. Either way both of those two approaches are made in the faith of feeling better, feeling LOVED. Aha!

However, when we base our decisions and actions in fear we become very tense and worried and end up wasting a lot of our time dwelling on decision making, placing our precious energy into the hands of people that we might not even really care about (or whom don't care about us) or even worse we place our happiness in the hands of something that may never ever happen. Damn.

So how do we change it? How do we start to move from a space of love?

Today my love, I want to share with you the most ancient secrets of all:

"WHATEVER YOU DECIDE TO DO OR NOT TO DO YOU ARE ALREADY LOVED"

did you hear me? Like REALLY hear me?!!

Ill say it again: "WHATEVER YOU DECIDE TO DO OR NOT TO DO YOU ARE ALREADY LOVED"

WOW. Once you truly grasp this truth there is no longer any need to stay fear based: you are already loveable and whole so whatever happens or doesn't happen does not change this beautiful, empowering fact. YOU ARE ALREADY TOTALLY AMAZING AND WORTHY.

So now, if you really get this skip the rest of the book and go on living your life to the max knowing YOU ARE ALREADY WORTHY OF EVERYTHING YOU DESIRE AND THAT LIFE LOVES YOU AND SUPPORTS YOUR DECISIONS 100%.

YEAH:)

However if you are still a bit doubtful (like the rest of humanity) please continue your 30 Day Morning Miracle Journey. I promise you this new truth will start to settle and become part of your core believes in good time, but for now keep up the good work:)

Love xx Josephine

Now to the off to perform the Morning Miracles we go!!

Step 1 Space :

Go to your special place where you start YOUR day. Sitting down make yourself comfortable in the ways that you know best with your favourite scented candle, incense, music or nothing but sacred silence- up to you.

Step 2 Breathe & Check In:

Close your eyes (NOT NOW OBVS). Place your hands on your heart. Breathe in deeply "I see you", exhale "I love you". Repeat for 2mins.

Pay close attention to ALL that may come up for you: all that your feeling, thinking and sensing just invite it all to flow through you.

Then start to ask yourself as you inhale: "how do I feel"? As you exhale allow the answer to land. Continue here for another 5 breaths. Stay open to how the answer may arrive: an image, a colour, a feeling, a voice, a memory these are all valid and equally important for you today. Now that you know a little bit more about how you are actually feeling at this moment in time move your hands down to your stomach: breathe in "what do I need?" Exhale allow that answer to land, continue here for another 5 breaths.

Step 3 High Vibes :

Now that you know whats really going on, what dialogue your mind is currently listening to we can take mindful actions to FINETUNE your current mood into one of LOVE, EXPANSION and CELEBRATION. WHAT you say? Bare with me:

Think of someone you LOVE unconditionally (BIG points if it's yourself). Remember the colour of their eyes, the warm smile they always give you, their scent, the last time you saw them. What did you do together? What time of day was it? What season? What were YOU wearing? How did it feel when they hugged YOU? That wonderful nourishing feeling of love starting at the heart spreading down all the way through to the toes and down through the arms and hands. Listen to their words now as they tell you how much YOU mean to them. How YOU are an inspiration in their life, how just knowing that YOU are apart of them makes them swell with love and pride.... THATS it beauty... NOW YOU GOT IT.... stay there. Close your eyes fall in love...stay there. Deep breath in, feeling all this love swirling around inside of you, when you are ready to exhale send ALL of your love right back to them thanking them for being in your life.

Step 4 Day Planning / Intention setting :

From this place of unconditional LOVE look at your day:

What simple steps can you make towards your dream today? Choose 3 things and write them here hehe yep YOU DECIDE which steps babe!! WHY YOU?!! Because YOU ARE THE ONLY ONE THAT KNOWS YOU! 123 GO:

1

2

3

Thats it!!! How simple was that? And it took you like 10mins???Out of your entire day!!

Now one tiny little thing and then your off;)

(Promise)!!

Step 5 Inspiration:

Write down 5 facts that proves to you that you are loved. Then return to look at them any time you forget your own worth GO:

1

2

3

4

5

Day 15 Forgiveness doesn't mean acceptance

Good morning beautiful and welcome to day 15:)

Whoop whoop we are half way through!! I am so grateful that YOU have chosen to be here with me every morning. To take this time out just for YOU.

Remember the importance of the very first 17secs of your day and how it sets the entire tune for your day? Good! Here is to another wonderful 2 weeks of even greater transformation and elevation!!

YOU are rising my love!!! Always remember this: every day YOU decide to start your day in this most empowered way by YOU putting AMAZING energy into YOU (yep these morning rituals are literally like food for your soul!) you will be fully equipped to face the day-whatever today brings you.

You are ATTRACTING into your life today exactly that which you are sending out! Wanna experience more joy? You must choose to look for, find, and then reconnect to the joy within yourself first. Want to be forgiven/able to forgive another? It starts by YOU forgiven yourself! Everything starts in YOU!

"As you forgive you are forgiven. As you decide to love and act lovingly towards yourself others will respond with love towards you. Everything starts in and with YOU"

Let's get started; we have amazing energy work to do!

All my love to you, I am SOOO proud of you!

xxx Josephine

Enjoy your Morning Rituals:

Step 1 Space :

Go to your special place where you start YOUR day. Sitting down make yourself comfortable in the ways that you know best with your favourite scented candle, incense, music or nothing but sacred silence- up to you.

Step 2 Breathe & Check In:

Close your eyes (NOT NOW OBVS). Place your hands on your heart. Breathe in deeply "I see you", exhale "I love you". Repeat for 2mins.

Pay close attention to ALL that may come up for you: all that your feeling, thinking and sensing just invite it all to flow through you.

Then start to ask yourself as you inhale: "how do I feel"? As you exhale allow the answer to land. Continue here for another 5 breaths. Stay open to how the answer may arrive: an image, a color, a feeling, a voice, a memory these are all valid and equally important for you today. Now that you know a little bit more about how you are actually feeling at this moment in time move your hands down to your stomach: breathe in "what do I need?" Exhale allow that answer to land, continue here for another 5 breaths.

Step 3 High Vibes :

Now that you know whats really going on, what dialogue your mind is currently listening to we can take mindful actions to FINETUNE your current mood into one of LOVE, EXPANSION and CELEBRATION. WHAT you say? Bare with me:

Think of someone you LOVE unconditionally (BIG points if it's yourself). Remember the colour of their eyes, the warm smile they always give you, their scent, the last time you saw them. What did

you do together? What time of day was it? What season? What were YOU wearing? How did it feel when they hugged YOU? That wonderful nourishing feeling of love starting at the heart spreading down all the way through to the toes and down through the arms and hands. Listen to their words now as they tell you how much YOU mean to them. How YOU are an inspiration in their life, how just knowing that YOU are apart of them makes them swell with love and pride.... THATS it beauty... NOW YOU GOT IT.... stay there. Close your eyes fall in love...stay there. Deep breath in, feeling all this love swirling around inside of you, when you are ready to exhale send ALL of your love right back to them thanking them for being in your life.

Step 4 Day Planning / Intention Setting :

From this place of unconditional LOVE look at your day:

What simple steps can you make towards your dream today? Choose 3 things and write them here hehe yep YOU DECIDE which steps babe!! WHY YOU?!! Because YOU ARE THE ONLY ONE THAT KNOWS YOU! 123 GO:

1

2

3

Thats it!!! How simple was that? And it took you like 10mins???Out of your entire day!!

Now one tiny little thing and then your off;)

(Promise)!!

Step 5 Inspiration:

Throughout your day stay curious: whatever comes up breathe deeply and keep on asking yourself: who/what am I ready to forgive?

Tonight give yourself 5-10mins before bed to reflect back over your day and write down any thoughts/ideas that came up. Then place your hand on your heart, close your eyes, remember everything that came up for you today...feel it...breathe into it...visualise it...then finally when YOU ARE READY TO FREE YOURSELF AND MOVE ON: call upon the angels, spirit guides etc- who ever you connect with - and say out loud:

"I see you and I love you, I see you and I forgive you. As I forgive I am forgiven. I am free and you are free and all is well." Repeat this until you feel calm and relaxed. And tomorrow when you wake up write down any dream/thoughts/feelings you had.

You are ready to let go of the old hurtful stories!! And the time is simply NOW my love!

Day 16 Just breathe

Good morning amazing soul,

Welcome to this new beautiful day!!

Today I invite you to pay close attention to your greatest gift of all: your breath.

So often we take it for granted... and yet the minute we no longer have it we get very aware of its miraculous purpose;)

The only thing we ever truly need in this life is our breath! Once we recognise, and utilise the power of breath, our life takes on a whole other meaning- things that seem to worry us no longer do so much, we get more energy and become balanced of mind, body and soul.

By breathing consciously throughout the day we are literally changing the alchemy of our bodies: the biochemistry changes when we breathe deeply (all the way into the belly) in and out. The PH levels in our body balances; goes from being or leaning towards acidic towards alkaline which means just by breathing we are literally reducing any current inflammation and prevent new inflammation from happening.

"The breathe is our medicine"

We are reducing and easing away STRESS.

All by breathing.

The breath is the key to our happiness, wellness and our liberation -

just like the ancient yogi's told us.

Today pay close attention to how you feel and whenever you notice a drop in energy or feel yourself triggered return to your breath:

place a hand on your belly and one on your heart inhaling deeply for a count of 5, followed by exhaling for a count of 10 (or 8/9).

The breath that dances through you is your greatest companion, your greatest teacher and your greatest doctor. Return to your breath- you can trust it.

Have a beautiful day my love,

xxxxxJosephine

And now it's time for your gorgeous Morning Rituals to begin...:

Step 1 Space :

Go to your special place where you start YOUR day. Sitting down make yourself comfortable in the ways that you know best with your favourite scented candle, incense, music or nothing but sacred silence- up to you.

Step 2 Breathe & Check In:

Close your eyes (NOT NOW OBVS). Place your hands on your heart. Breathe in deeply "I see you", exhale "I love you". Repeat for 2mins.

Pay close attention to ALL that may come up for you: all that your feeling, thinking and sensing just invite it all to flow through you.

Then start to ask yourself as you inhale: "how do I feel"? As you exhale allow the answer to land. Continue here for another 5 breaths. Stay open to how the answer may arrive: an image, a colour, a feeling, a voice, a memory these are all valid and equally important for you today. Now that you know a little bit more about how you are actually feeling at this moment in time move your hands down to your stomach: breathe in "what do I need?" Exhale allow that answer to land, continue here for another 5 breaths.

Step 3 High Vibes :

Now that you know whats really going on, what dialogue your mind is currently listening to we can take mindful actions to FINETUNE your current mood into one of LOVE, EXPANSION and CELEBRATION. WHAT you say? Bare with me:

Think of someone you LOVE unconditionally (BIG points if it's yourself). Remember the colour of their eyes, the warm smile they always give you, their scent, the last time you saw them. What did you do together? What time of day was it? What season? What were YOU wearing? How did it feel when they hugged YOU? That wonderful nourishing feeling of love starting at the heart spreading down all the way through to the toes and down through the arms and hands. Listen to their words now as they tell you how much YOU mean to them. How YOU are an inspiration in their life, how just knowing that YOU are apart of them makes them swell with love and pride.... THATS it beauty... NOW YOU GOT IT.... stay there. Close your eyes fall in love...stay there. Deep breath in, feeling all this love swirling around inside of you, when you are ready to exhale send ALL of your love right back to them thanking them for being in your life.

Step 4 Day Planning / Intention Setting :

From this place of unconditional LOVE look at your day:

What simple steps can you make towards your dream today? Choose 3 things and write them here hehe yep YOU DECIDE which steps babe!! WHY YOU?!! Because YOU ARE THE ONLY ONE THAT KNOWS YOU! 123 GO:

1

2

3

Thats it!!! How simple was that? And it took you like 10mins???Out of your entire day!!

Now one tiny little thing and then your off;)

(Promise)!!

Step 5 Inspiration:

As you go about your day remember to take some beautiful deep, slow breaths and notice how these bring you into this wonderful space of calm, peace and ease. Especially use this whenever you feel out of balance or before you make a big decision. Then, tonight before bed, write down in your journal how, when and why you decided to use the tool of breath and in doing so how it help you return back to you!! All we ever truly need is the breath that fills our being with positivity and joy.

Day 17 What would you do if you knew you couldn't fail?

Good morning my love,

Have you ever thought about how your life would look or feel if you knew, deep at your inner core, that you couldn't fail? That whatever you set your mind to would ONLY ever bring you even closer to living in full alignment with your truth?

Think about it for a moment... What do you desire more than anything in the world right now? Breathe into that for a moment.

Now, whilst you keep on breathing listen to my words: You are a child of the universe, you are made from the same stars that shine down upon us, you have the earth, the waters, the fire, space and air inside you. Everything that you see and experience around you is already within you. And therefore you, yourself, as much as everyone else is 100% capable of achieving whatever you set your mind too: what you desire is made from the same elements and energy as you, so it is only completely natural that you already have what it takes to make your wishes manifest. Ie if you already have all of the ingredients to bake a wonderful, warming cardamom cake, well then you CAN bake a wonderful, warming cardamom cake! Now you may think: But Josie I don't know the recipe!!! No my love again not true- You have the recipe inside of you, only you have been thinking for wayyyy too long that you didn't.

"The greatest fear is not that we are inadequate, the greatest fear is that we are powerful beyond measure"

Use this wisdom today to bring YOU back to YOU.

Love Josephine

Time to start your Morning Rituals:

Step 1 Space :

Go to your special place where you start YOUR day. Sitting down make yourself comfortable in the ways that you know best with your favourite scented candle, incense, music or nothing but sacred silence- up to you.

Step 2 Breathe & Check In:

Close your eyes (NOT NOW OBVS). Place your hands on your heart. Breathe in deeply "I see you", exhale "I love you". Repeat for 2mins.

Pay close attention to ALL that may come up for you: all that your feeling, thinking and sensing just invite it all to flow through you.

Then start to ask yourself as you inhale: "how do I feel"? As you exhale allow the answer to land. Continue here for another 5 breaths. Stay open to how the answer may arrive: an image, a color, a feeling, a voice, a memory these are all valid and equally important for you today. Now that you know a little bit more about how you are actually feeling at this moment in time move your hands down to your stomach: breathe in "what do I need?" Exhale allow that answer to land, continue here for another 5 breaths.

Step 3 High Vibes :

Now that you know whats really going on, what dialogue your mind is currently listening to we can take mindful actions to FINETUNE your current mood into one of LOVE, EXPANSION and CELEBRATION. WHAT you say? Bare with me:

Think of someone you LOVE unconditionally (BIG points if it's yourself). Remember the colour of their eyes, the warm smile they always give you, their scent, the last time you saw them. What did you do together? What time of day was it? What season? What were YOU wearing? How did it feel when they hugged YOU? That wonderful nourishing feeling of love starting at the heart spreading down all the way through to the toes and down through the arms and hands. Listen to their words now as they tell you how much YOU mean to them. How YOU are an inspiration in their life, how just knowing that YOU are apart of them makes them swell with love and pride.... THATS it beauty... NOW YOU GOT IT.... stay there. Close your eyes fall in love...stay there. Deep breath in, feeling all this love swirling around inside of you, when you are ready to exhale send ALL of your love right back to them thanking them for being in your life.

Step 4 Day Planning / Intention Setting :

From this place of unconditional LOVE look at your day:

What simple steps can you make towards your dream today? Choose 3 things and write them here hehe yep YOU DECIDE which steps babe!! WHY YOU?!! Because YOU ARE THE ONLY ONE THAT KNOWS YOU! 123 GO:

1

2

3

Thats it!!! How simple was that? And it took you like 10mins???Out of your entire day!!

Now one tiny little thing and then your off;)

(Promise)!!

Step 5 Inspiration:

I invite you to visualise YOUR IDEAL happy life and focus on how it makes you feel in the body. Do this with your eyes closed so your HEART and soul have space to speak.

Write down 3 things such as feelings, sensations and images that come up for you during this visualisation:

1

2

3

Day 18 Just Show Up

Welcome to this new day beautiful soul,

This morning I want to remind you that the greatest thing we can ever do for ourself, our dreams, anyone or anything else, is to simply show up!

Nothing is going to change if you just think about change: not your life experience, not how you feel, not your energy levels nada nothing!

But lasting changes don't happen over night just like Rome wasn't build in a day. The ONLY thing that you truly ever need to do is SHOW UP – and KEEP ON SHOWING UP.

So my love you are already there: as you decided to SHOW UP THIS MORNING!!

Yeah go you!!

Take a moment to really celebrate this: Im sure there were many other things and ideas asking for your attention this morning? Many other "voices" in your mind telling you why you couldn't and shouldn't possibly be taking this time out just for you? Hmmm yes it happens to us all. However YOU decided to prioritise YOU this morning. You cut through the bullshit and remembered who you are and why you came to be here: you remembered your purpose, and guided and driven by this, decided to reconnect to YOU. You decided to JUST SHOW UP.

However you feel on any given day or moment just show up. How ever many reasons your mind will give you NOT to go- just show up.

Keep on showing up. It's through COMMITTING to your dreams, to your GREATEST health and wealth on all levels that your life IS transforming.

And that my love simply makes YOU one hell of an awesome being. Now let's get to work!!

Love xx Josephine

Morning Miracle time hip,hip hoorah:

Step 1 Space :

Go to your special place where you start YOUR day. Sitting down make yourself comfortable in the ways that you know best with your favourite scented candle, incense, music or nothing but sacred silence- up to you.

Step 2 Breathe & Check In:

Close your eyes (NOT NOW OBVS). Place your hands on your heart. Breathe in deeply "I see you", exhale "I love you". Repeat for 2mins.

Pay close attention to ALL that may come up for you: all that your feeling, thinking and sensing just invite it all to flow through you.

Then start to ask yourself as you inhale: "how do I feel"? As you exhale allow the answer to land. Continue here for another 5 breaths. Stay open to how the answer may arrive: an image, a colour, a feeling, a voice, a memory these are all valid and equally important for you today. Now that you know a little bit more about how you are actually feeling at this moment in time move your hands down to your stomach: breathe in "what do I need?" Exhale allow that answer to land, continue here for another 5 breaths.

Step 3 High Vibes :

Now that you know whats really going on, what dialogue your mind is currently listening to we can take mindful actions to FINETUNE your current mood into one of LOVE, EXPANSION and CELEBRATION. WHAT you say? Bare with me:

Think of someone you LOVE unconditionally (BIG points if it's yourself). Remember the colour of their eyes, the warm smile they always give you, their scent, the last time you saw them. What did you do together? What time of day was it? What season? What were YOU wearing? How did it feel when they hugged YOU? That wonderful nourishing feeling of love starting at the heart spreading down all the way through to the toes and down through the arms and hands. Listen to their words now as they tell you how much YOU mean to them. How YOU are an inspiration in their life, how just knowing that YOU are a part of them makes them swell with love and pride.... THATS it beauty... NOW YOU GOT IT.... stay there. Close your eyes fall in love...stay there. Deep breath in, feeling all this love swirling around inside of you, when you are ready to exhale send ALL of your love right back to them thanking them for being in your life.

Step 4 Day Planning / Intention Setting :

From this place of unconditional LOVE look at your day:

What simple steps can you make towards your dream today? Choose 3 things and write them here hehe yep YOU DECIDE which steps babe!! WHY YOU?!! Because YOU ARE THE ONLY ONE THAT KNOWS YOU! 123 GO:

1

2

3

Thats it!!! How simple was that? And it took you like 10mins???Out of your entire day!!

Now one tiny little thing and then your off;)

(Promise)!!

Step 5 Inspiration:

I invite you to visualise YOUR IDEAL happy life and focus on how it makes you feel in the body. Do this with your eyes closed so your HEART and soul have space to speak.

Write down 3 things such as feelings, sensations and images that come up for you during this visualisation:

1

2

3

Day 19 The law of love

Good morning lovely,

Without sounding too airy fairy I want you to know another universal fact:

There is an abundance of love at all times throughout all space across all planes. This is important for you to grasp so I will say it again:

"There is an abundance of love at all times throughout all of space, across all planes"

So you never need worry that you might run out of love, or somehow be late for the love quota when the universe is handing it out. There is ALWAYS an ever flowing, continual abundance of love everywhere, where ever you go.

It exists within you and all around you. Always! Even on days where you are doubting yourself and your abilities.

All though most of us can't see it with our eyes, you CAN train your heart to be able to feel it. In fact I think you already know that don't you? Isn't that what you have been feeling more and more the last few days? As you get up that little earlier to make time for YOU, by setting yourself up for a wonderful, magical inspiring day? Haven't you felt this love when you walked down the street and noticed how more and more people every day are greeting you with smiles and hallo's? Haven't you noticed how you have so much more energy than usual- even in the late afternoons? Well my love it is not because there is somehow more love in the air- it is because you, as you are now CHOOSING to pay attention to it, can feel how the whole world is filled with love, light and positivity. The only one who is changing here is YOU my love. Life itself, the Universe, has always been sending you love. Always been here, looking after you; when you were asleep, at work at home, happy, sad overwhelmed etc. The Universe is constantly supplying all of us with an ABUNDANCE of love! Because it believes in us. Because we are made from the same fabric that created the Universe: because we too are LOVE. In the words of Albert Einstein:

"If we are to save the world and all of its inhabitants the one and only answer has always been, and will always be, love"

Love is a science that when used correctly will energise you, inspire you and allow you to create and manifest any and all of your dreams. Now let's begin this day:)

Love xx Josephine

Morning Rituals time:

Step 1 Space :

Go to your special place where you start YOUR day. Sitting down make yourself comfortable in the ways that you know best with your favourite scented candle, incense, music or nothing but sacred silence- up to you.

Step 2 Breathe & Check In:

Close your eyes (NOT NOW OBVS). Place your hands on your heart. Breathe in deeply "I see you", exhale "I love you". Repeat for 2mins.

Pay close attention to ALL that may come up for you: all that your feeling, thinking and sensing just invite it all to flow through you.

Then start to ask yourself as you inhale: "how do I feel"? As you exhale allow the answer to land. Continue here for another 5 breaths. Stay open to how the answer may arrive: an image, a color, a feeling, a voice, a memory these are all valid and equally important for you today. Now that you know a little bit more about how you are actually feeling at this moment in time move your hands down to your stomach: breathe in "what do I need?" Exhale allow that answer to land, continue here for another 5 breaths.

Step 3 High Vibes :

Now that you know whats really going on, what dialogue your mind is currently listening to we can take mindful actions to FINETUNE your current mood into one of LOVE, EXPANSION and CELEBRATION. WHAT you say? Bare with me:

Think of someone you LOVE unconditionally (BIG points if it's yourself). Remember the colour of their eyes, the warm smile they always give you, their scent, the last time you saw them. What did you do together? What time of day was it? What season? What were YOU wearing? How did it feel when they hugged YOU? That wonderful nourishing feeling of love starting at the heart spreading down all the way through to the toes and down through the arms and hands. Listen to their words now as they tell you how much YOU mean to them. How YOU are an inspiration in their life, how just knowing that YOU are a part of them makes them swell with love and pride.... THATS it beauty... NOW YOU GOT IT.... stay there. Close your eyes fall in love...stay there. Deep breath in, feeling all this love swirling around inside of you, when you are ready to exhale send ALL of your love right back to them thanking them for being in your life.

Step 4 Day Planning / Intention Setting :

From this place of unconditional LOVE look at your day:

What simple steps can you make towards your dream today? Choose

3 things and write them here hehe yep YOU DECIDE which steps babe!! WHY YOU?!! Because YOU ARE THE ONLY ONE THAT KNOWS YOU! 123 GO:

1

2

3

Thats it!!! How simple was that? And it took you like 10mins???Out of your entire day!!

Now one tiny little thing and then your off;)

(Promise)!!

Step 5 Inspiration:

I invite you to visualise YOUR IDEAL happy life and focus on how it makes you feel in the body. Do this with your eyes closed so your HEART and soul have space to speak.

Write down 3 things such as feelings, sensations and images that come up for you during this visualisation:

1

2

3

Day 20 Deep listening

Good morning beautiful being of light and love,

Welcome to this gorgeous new day, take a moment to really INVITE in the energy of this brand new day that has come upon us, remembering that this day is filled with endless positive opportunities. Extend your arms out away from your body and open your mind, heart and body, welcoming in this beautiful new day with the words: THANK YOU, THANK YOU, THANK YOU!!!!

When we start each day with giving thanks we tune into the frequency of gratitude and that heightens our own energy and vibration setting us up for an incredible day. Today I want you to remember that everything is connected: that there is NO separation between mind, body and soul: you, me and the world: planet Earth, Venus or the Universe... We are never alone we are all one.

With this in mind, I invite you to pay special attention to what your body, including all of your senses, is telling you. Your body has a deep inner wisdom that in many ways greatly overrides that of the brain. Unfortunately many have become so dependant on using only their brain and the information coming in through the eyes that they have simply forgotten to ask the rest of the body for help.

Your body is made out of a magnificent collection of 50 trillion cells and each of them are constantly feeling and sensing all that goes on-outside and inside. Your cells pick up on the vibration of love or danger much faster than your brain ever will. Your body always knows the way, and your body keeps the score: whatever happens in your life is stored not only as memories in your brain, but throughout your entire body. Ever wondered what that pain which appears out of "no where" and which comes and goes sporadically is all about? Even had a physiotherapist look at it, but everything seemed fine? Your body remembers every single time you felt happy, sad, loved, scared etc etc. And all of these experiences have left an imprint on your physical and emotional body as well as on your mind.

Remember that the body is always on your side no matter what happens ie if you loose a leg your body will make the necessary adjustments and go on living without as much as a hmmm "Im not sure I want to look after you anymore!" ie YOU CAN ALWAYS TRUST YOUR BODY, it is on your side!! Make peace with your body today! Listen to what it has to say and when ever something is out of balance place a hand on that place and ask: "WHAT IS THIS TEACHING ME? HOW CAN I BEST SUPPORT THE JOURNEY? IM SORRY AND I LOVE YOU".

Once you fully grasp this miraculous truth you will be able to HEAL YOURSELF. Just like that!

And I know you are already well on your way, otherwise you simply would not be here to day!!! So my love, if your ready to start HEALING lets begin your Morning Rituals:

Step 1 Space :

Go to your special place where you start YOUR day. Sitting down make yourself comfortable in the ways that you know best with your favourite scented candle, incense, music or nothing but sacred silence- up to you.

Step 2 Breathe & Check In:

Close your eyes (NOT NOW OBVS). Place your hands on your heart. Breathe in deeply "I see you", exhale "I love you". Repeat for 2mins.

Pay close attention to ALL that may come up for you: all that your feeling, thinking and sensing just invite it all to flow through you.

Then start to ask yourself as you inhale: "how do I feel"? As you exhale allow the answer to land. Continue here for another 5 breaths. Stay open to how the answer may arrive: an image, a colour, a feeling, a voice, a memory these are all valid and equally important for you today. Now that you know a little bit more about how you are actually feeling at this moment in time move your hands down to your stomach: breathe in "what do I need?" Exhale allow that answer to land, continue here for another 5 breaths.

Step 3 High Vibes :

Now that you know whats really going on, what dialogue your mind is currently listening to we can take mindful actions to FINETUNE your current mood into one of LOVE, EXPANSION and CELEBRATION. WHAT you say? Bare with me:

Think of someone you LOVE unconditionally (BIG points if it's yourself). Remember the colour of their eyes, the warm smile they always give you, their scent, the last time you saw them. What did you do together? What time of day was it? What season? What were YOU wearing? How did it feel when they hugged YOU? That wonderful nourishing feeling of love starting at the heart spreading down all the way through to the toes and down through the arms and hands. Listen to their words now as they tell you how much YOU mean to them. How YOU are an inspiration in their life, how just knowing that YOU are a part of them makes them swell with love and pride.... THATS it beauty... NOW YOU GOT IT.... stay there. Close your eyes fall in love...stay there. Deep breath in, feeling all this love swirling around inside of you, when you are ready to exhale send ALL of your love right back to them thanking them for being in your life.

Step 4 Day Planning / Intention Setting :

From this place of unconditional LOVE look at your day:

What simple steps can you make towards your dream today? Choose 3 things and write them here hehe yep YOU DECIDE which steps babe!! WHY YOU?!! Because YOU ARE THE ONLY ONE THAT KNOWS YOU! 123 GO:

1

2

3

Thats it!!! How simple was that? And it took you like 10mins???Out of your entire day!!

Now one tiny little thing and then your off;)

(Promise)!!

Step 5 Inspiration:

Write down how your body usually signals you need to take some time out below:

1

2

3

4

5

6

7

8

9

10

11

12

Do you get head aches? Pain in the lower back or digestive issues etc? Listen to your body and honour what it has to say, so that next time when this happens you will approach these reactions from a space of love and curiosity asking your body "What are you teaching me? How can I best support this journey? Im sorry I couldn't look after you better, I LOVE you"

"Your body is always on your side. Your body loves you"

Day 21 Move

Good morning beautiful soul,

Welcome to this fantastic day!! Today marks a 3 week cycle wow check you out! Take a moment to reflect back to the day you first decided to embark on this journey. What made you commit to The 30 Day Morning Miracle? Which dreams were drawing you into this adventure?

Remembering your WHY each and every day is what has been propelling you into taking full responsibility for your own happiness and the reason why you are feeling better and better as you get deeper into this transformational process. The only one responsible for this rejuvenation is YOU my love!!! So well done!!!

Now the next thing is to understand that EVERYTHING in our universe MOVES. On a cellular level everything is moving- all though to the physical eye our surroundings including our own bodies look dense and separate from one another, the truth, which we see when we look through a microscope, is that everything is constantly moving: cells, atoms, nature, people, animals, furniture etc etc everything is moving! Emotions literally mean energy in motion.

"So my love the KEY to your success on any level, whatever it is that YOU desire, is to keep on moving"

Every day, step by step, do a little towards your dreams, every day MOVE towards your dreams. Move your body (doesn't matter so much how you move but that you move), every day MOVE your mind (read something that really expands your mind, remember the brain is a muscle so keep on moving that muscle), every day, however you feel emotionally allow those emotions to stay in motion by expressing yourself truthfully and freely (through creative endeavours, journaling, singing dancing, talking etc).

Whatever you do keep on MOVING.

Throughout your day today keep on asking yourself "where am I stagnant/ where am I ready to move on"? Reflect on your work, personal life, dreams, home, belief systems, people and spaces. Keep declaring to yourself and the Universe: " I am ready to move on. I allow life to love me. I am moved by life"

And on that note it's time for your Morning Rituals:

Step 1 Space :

Go to your special place where you start YOUR day. Sitting down make yourself comfortable in the ways that you know best with your favourite scented candle, incense, music or nothing but sacred silence- up to you.

Step 2 Breathe & Check In:

Close your eyes (NOT NOW OBVS). Place your hands on your heart. Breathe in deeply "I see you", exhale "I love you". Repeat for 2mins.

Pay close attention to ALL that may come up for you: all that your feeling, thinking and sensing just invite it all to flow through you.

Then start to ask yourself as you inhale: "how do I feel"? As you exhale allow the answer to land. Continue here for another 5 breaths. Stay open to how the answer may arrive: an image, a colour, a feeling, a voice, a memory these are all valid and equally important for you today. Now that you know a little bit more about how you are actually feeling at this moment in time move your hands down to your stomach: breathe in "what do I need?" Exhale allow that answer to land, continue here for another 5 breaths.

Step 3 High Vibes :

Now that you know whats really going on, what dialogue your mind is currently listening to we can take mindful actions to FINETUNE your current mood into one of LOVE, EXPANSION and CELEBRATION. WHAT you say? Bare with me:

Think of someone you LOVE unconditionally (BIG points if it's yourself). Remember the colour of their eyes, the warm smile they always give you, their scent, the last time you saw them. What did you do together? What time of day was it? What season? What were YOU wearing? How did it feel when they hugged YOU? That wonderful nourishing feeling of love starting at the heart spreading down all the way through to the toes and down through the arms and hands. Listen to their words now as they tell you how much YOU mean to them. How YOU are an inspiration in their life, how just knowing that YOU are a part of them makes them swell with love and pride.... THATS it beauty... NOW YOU GOT IT.... stay there. Close your eyes fall in love...stay there. Deep breath in, feeling all this love swirling around inside of you, when you are ready to exhale send ALL of your love right back to them thanking them for being in your life.

Step 4 Day Planning / Intention Setting :

From this place of unconditional LOVE look at your day:

What simple steps can you make towards your dream today? Choose 3 things and write them here hehe yep YOU DECIDE which steps babe!! WHY YOU?!! Because YOU ARE THE ONLY ONE THAT KNOWS YOU! 123 GO:

1

2

3

Thats it!!! How simple was that? And it took you like 10mins???Out of your entire day!!

Now one tiny little thing and then your off;)

(Promise)!!

Step 5 Inspiration:

In what ways and areas could you see yourself benefit from MOVING MORE / MOVING ON? Write them down now and give them a date and a time so you know you are 100% committed to these changes:

1

2

3

Day 22 Rewrite your story

Good morning my love and welcome to day 22 'Rewrite your story'.

This is one of the most empowering tools we have! Only we get to decide how we wish to remember our upbringing, our family, our work and personal life. Only we have the power to let whatever happens be what makes us or breaks us. Only we have that power!!

So my love, this morning I invite you to look back at your life from the day you were born up until this very moment and write down everything you remember (you can do this as detailed or as roughly as you like!). Once you have finished check if you left anything out? Either that which made you feel amazing, like an amazing success, or any painful, challenging memories? Now also look at which words you have used to describe YOUR STORY!! Are they empowering? Or disempowering ie are you the hero/heroine or victim of your story?

"The only one that ever get to choose how the past impacts our TODAY and TOMORROW is us!!!"

YOU my love!!

Ask yourself: am I ready to take full responsibility for whatever happened? Am I ready to decide to LEARN from every single experience life brings me? However hard, however wonderful, am I finally ready to look for the blessings within the lessons?

Ask yourself 'What is reality made of?' and the answer is simple: Only that which YOU hold true!!!

The ONLY truth that ever exist is what you belief in!
Anything can be positive or negative- it ALWAYS just depends what side of the coin you look at!!!!
The only TRUTH that exists is what YOU value/ where you focus!!!
Rewrite your story today my love, you have been feeling small for way too long!

Rewrite your most empowered, uplifting story including ALL that took place but seen from an empowered angle asking yourself 'what did this teach me'? 'How did it make me stronger wiser and kinder than ever before'?
CHOOSE how you see your past!
It is time to rise.

Love Josephine

Let's begin your Morning Rituals!

Step 1 Space :

Go to your special place where you start YOUR day. Sitting down make yourself comfortable in the ways that you know best with your favourite scented candle, incense, music or nothing but sacred silence- up to you.

Step 2 Breathe & Check In:

Close your eyes (NOT NOW OBVS). Place your hands on your heart. Breathe in deeply "I see you", exhale "I love you". Repeat for 2mins.

Pay close attention to ALL that may come up for you: all that your feeling, thinking and sensing just invite it all to flow through you.

Then start to ask yourself as you inhale: "how do I feel"? As you exhale allow the answer to land. Continue here for another 5 breaths. Stay open to how the answer may arrive: an image, a colour, a feeling, a voice, a memory these are all valid and equally important for you today. Now that you know a little bit more about how you are actually feeling at this moment in time move your hands down to your stomach: breathe in "what do I need?" Exhale allow that answer to land, continue here for another 5 breaths.

Step 3 High Vibes :

Now that you know whats really going on, what dialogue your mind is currently listening to we can take mindful actions to FINETUNE your current mood into one of LOVE, EXPANSION and CELEBRATION. WHAT you say? Bare with me:

Think of someone you LOVE unconditionally (BIG points if it's yourself). Remember the colour of their eyes, the warm smile they always give you, their scent, the last time you saw them. What did you do together? What time of day was it? What season? What were YOU wearing? How did it feel when they hugged YOU? That wonderful nourishing feeling of love starting at the heart spreading down all the way through to the toes and down through the arms and hands. Listen to their words now as they tell you how much YOU mean to them. How YOU are an inspiration in their life, how just knowing that YOU are a part of them makes them swell with love and pride.... THATS it beauty... NOW YOU GOT IT.... stay there. Close your eyes fall in love...stay there. Deep breath in, feeling all this love swirling around inside of you, when you are ready to exhale send ALL of your love right back to them thanking them for being in your life.

Step 4 Day Planning / Intention Setting :

From this place of unconditional LOVE look at your day:

What simple steps can you make towards your dream today? Choose 3 things and write them here hehe yep YOU DECIDE which steps babe!! WHY YOU?!! Because YOU ARE THE ONLY ONE THAT KNOWS YOU! 123 GO:

1

2

3

Thats it!!! How simple was that? And it took you like 10mins???Out of your entire day!!

Now one tiny little thing and then your off;)

(Promise)!!

Step 5 Inspiration:

Write down your new empowered life story (the one where you CHOOSE to see everything as a blessing). Feel free to continue in your journal if you run out of space.

Day 23 The law of change

Good morning amazing being of love and light,

Welcome to day 23 'The law of change'.

Today I want to share with you how and why everything in our entire Universe changes and how important it is to allow these changes to occur. To embrace and embody change. The art of letting go with grace. Letting go of outcomes... it is our resistance to change, to the unknown, to not being in charge that causes us the suffering not the actual things themselves.

"The only thing that is ever certain is change"

When we look at Nature this is so evidenced: Summer turns to Fall, Fall to Winter and so on. Night turns into day. People animals, plant and flowers are created and manifested; they grow and blossom (ascending energy) and one day this all changes as they start to return back to Mother Earth, slowly disintegrating and releasing their physical bodies (descending energy).

Change is what renews us:

The end of something is merely the BEGINNING of something new!

We have another Universal law that says 'What was once created in love will never seize to exist'. And with this we come to understand that nothing really ever dies- once energy is created it will always exist on some level - in one form or another.

So my love, today let's find comfort hope and inspiration in the law of change.

Let's honour our beautiful magical Universe that has created this incredible miracle for all of us to be part of. For all of us to change, move, evolve and rise together as one energy shifting from one form to another. The Universe it self is constantly changing and expanding; longs to realise its full potential just like we do.

Today lets embrace whatever changes we are currently going through or see around us remembering that the only way to fully evolve into whatever energy is needed for the highest good of all is to change!

Change doesn't have to mean worse; change is always the beginning of something more refined, better suited, more elevated for this moment in time...

Today ask yourself: where in my life am I ready to embrace change?

This can mean anything from decluttering your home/ or buying something new to starting a new nutritionally balanced diet, to leaving an old draining job or relationship behind etc etc.

Always ask yourself how and where can I embrace and embody change? For the only thing that is ever certain in our life is change.

I love you,   xxx Josephine

Let's commence your Morning Rituals:

Step 1 Space :

Go to your special place where you start YOUR day. Sitting down make yourself comfortable in the ways that you know best with your favourite scented candle, incense, music or nothing but sacred silence- up to you.

Step 2 Breathe & Check In:

Close your eyes (NOT NOW OBVS). Place your hands on your heart. Breathe in deeply "I see you", exhale "I love you". Repeat for 2mins.

Pay close attention to ALL that may come up for you: all that your feeling, thinking and sensing just invite it all to flow through you.

Then start to ask yourself as you inhale: "how do I feel"? As you exhale allow the answer to land. Continue here for another 5 breaths. Stay open to how the answer may arrive: an image, a colour, a feeling, a voice, a memory these are all valid and equally important for you today. Now that you know a little bit more about how you are actually feeling at this moment in time move your hands down to your stomach: breathe in "what do I need?" Exhale allow that answer to land, continue here for another 5 breaths.

Step 3 High Vibes :

Now that you know whats really going on, what dialogue your mind is currently listening to we can take mindful actions to FINETUNE your current mood into one of LOVE, EXPANSION and CELEBRATION. WHAT you say? Bare with me:

Think of someone you LOVE unconditionally (BIG points if it's yourself). Remember the colour of their eyes, the warm smile they always give you, their scent, the last time you saw them. What did you do together? What time of day was it? What season? What were YOU wearing? How did it feel when they hugged YOU? That wonderful nourishing feeling of love starting at the heart spreading down all the way through to the toes and down through the arms and hands. Listen to their words now as they tell you how much YOU mean to them. How YOU are an inspiration in their life, how just knowing that YOU are a part of them makes them swell with love and pride.... THATS it beauty... NOW YOU GOT IT.... stay there. Close your eyes fall in love...stay there. Deep breath in, feeling all this love swirling around inside of you, when you are ready to exhale send ALL of your love right back to them thanking them for being in your life.

Step 4 Day Planning / Intention Setting :

From this place of unconditional LOVE look at your day:

What simple steps can you make towards your dream today? Choose 3 things and write them here hehe yep YOU DECIDE which steps babe!! WHY YOU?!! Because YOU ARE THE ONLY ONE THAT KNOWS YOU! 123 GO:

1

2

3

Thats it!!! How simple was that? And it took you like 10mins???Out of your entire day!!

Now one tiny little thing and then your off;)

(Promise)!!

Step 5 Inspiration:

Ask yourself: "where in my life am I ready to change? To transform and to renew myself"?

Mentally, emotionally, physically and even spiritually.

Write your answers here:

Day 24 The law of manifestation

Good morning to you my magnificent soul,

Welcome to a new beautiful day filled with endless opportunities.

Let's take a deep breath in and consciously welcome in the renewed energy that this wonderful, special day brings us.

Let's decide that TODAY is the best day of our life!

Remember my love, everything in life is a CHOICE- especially positivity!!

Today I want to share with you the secret of manifestation: how and why it works. Together I will help you shed light in your own darkness to illuminate that which has been stopping you from fully creating and living your most wonderful dream life.

Since ancient times the wise ones told us, the stars, the angels, the moon, the Earth and the sun kept reminding us of this vital truth and yet somehow we managed to forget... somehow most of us neglected what was being shown to us over and over again. But TODAY I know you are ready to listen: I know you have been searching for so long... longing for inspiration... for a sign... anything that would confirm what your heart has been saying all along:

"what you seek is also seeking you"

My love, our entire Universe is but a reflection of your own energy and frequency. What you want to see and manifest "out there" must first and foremost be created and manifested "in here". Ie whatever it is that you most desire you must atune your own energy to match: if you want to attract a loving partner who adores and respects you, you yourself must first adore and respect yourself. You must BELIEVE that you can have and are worthy of ANYTHING you desire. If you desire a wonderful home with a gorgeous view of the ocean you must ask yourself how it would FEEL to live in that wonderful home and how it would FEEL to enjoy that gorgeous view of the ocean? The key to your success is in enquiring within, find the feeling you long for and then visualise and feel that energy within you and all around you at all times. Dont worry too much about how and when that home or that partner will come to you- focus ONLY on the feeling of already living there/ already being with that lovely partner. How do we do this in daily life you ask? Well if you believe that living in that home will make you feel a deep sense of freedom and joy then you must activate these emotions (set these energies in motions) every single day by doing whichever activities that activates exactly those emotions in you.

Everything starts in YOU. Stay connected to the feelings you belief you will have once your dreams manifest and you will literally be drawing in everything and everyone that matches your own vibration. Everything is energy remember? Forget about the details of how, if or when, and ONLY concern yourself with

step 1 ask for what you want step

2 feel into how that will feel to have/be

step 3 give all your worries to the Universe and let the Universe look after the details of how to get you what you dream of step

4 BELIEVE that you are 100% worthy and able to manifest your wildest dreams and only engage with people thoughts, words and activities that brings you into that highest state of energy: because

that feeling state is what draws all that you desire into existence.

Now my love, breathe in "I am a WONDERFUL human being" exhale out " I now release ALL else. All is well". Continue a few more times until you really feel your energy rising and your heart opening and softening.

You are a winner and I know you are going to ROCK at this. Keep a manifestation journal over the next 30 days and see what happens, pay special attention to how you FEEL and what you choose to do every single day in order to keep your vibe high!!!

The way to manifest is to stay in your highest, most divine energy every day!

I love you,

xxx Josephine

Now it's time for your Morning Rituals:

Step 1 Space :

Go to your special place where you start YOUR day. Sitting down make yourself comfortable in the ways that you know best with your favourite scented candle, incense, music or nothing but sacred silence- up to you.

Step 2 Breathe & Check In:

Close your eyes (NOT NOW OBVS). Place your hands on your heart. Breathe in deeply "I see you", exhale "I love you". Repeat for 2mins.

Pay close attention to ALL that may come up for you: all that your feeling, thinking and sensing just invite it all to flow through you.

Then start to ask yourself as you inhale: "how do I feel"? As you exhale allow the answer to land. Continue here for another 5 breaths.

Stay open to how the answer may arrive: an image, a colour, a feeling, a voice, a memory these are all valid and equally important for you today. Now that you know a little bit more about how you are actually feeling at this moment in time move your hands down to your stomach: breathe in "what do I need?" Exhale allow that answer to land, continue here for another 5 breaths.

Step 3 High Vibes :

Now that you know whats really going on, what dialogue your mind is currently listening to we can take mindful actions to FINETUNE your current mood into one of LOVE, EXPANSION and CELEBRATION. WHAT you say? Bare with me:

Think of someone you LOVE unconditionally (BIG points if it's yourself). Remember the colour of their eyes, the warm smile they always give you, their scent, the last time you saw them. What did you do together? What time of day was it? What season? What were YOU wearing? How did it feel when they hugged YOU? That wonderful nourishing feeling of love starting at the heart spreading down all the way through to the toes and down through the arms and hands. Listen to their words now as they tell you how much YOU mean to them. How YOU are an inspiration in their life, how just knowing that YOU are a part of them makes them swell with love and pride.... THATS it beauty... NOW YOU GOT IT.... stay there. Close your eyes fall in love...stay there. Deep breath in, feeling all this love swirling around inside of you, when you are ready to exhale send ALL of your love right back to them thanking them for being in your life.

Step 4 Day Planning / Intention Setting :

From this place of unconditional LOVE look at your day:

What simple steps can you make towards your dream today? Choose 3 things and write them here hehe yep YOU DECIDE which steps babe!! WHY YOU?!! Because YOU ARE THE ONLY ONE THAT

KNOWS YOU! 123 GO:

1

2

3

Thats it!!! How simple was that? And it took you like 10mins???Out of your entire day!!

Now one tiny little thing and then your off;)

(Promise)!!

Step 5 Inspiration:

I invite you to visualise YOUR IDEAL happy life and focus on how it makes you feel in the body. Do this with your eyes closed so your HEART and soul have space to speak.

Write down 3 things such as feelings, sensations and images that come up for you during this visualisation:

1

2

3

Day 25 Focus on joy

Dear heart,

Good morning my love, rise and shine let's celebrate that we are ALIVE. That we get to enjoy another beautiful day on this wonderful planet Earth. Today really focus on all that brings you JOY. Use all of your senses to really converse with Life herself. Use your eyes to really see and enjoy all of the incredible beautiful sights that will show themselves to you today: the smile of your loved ones, the beauty of nature: the trees, the flowers and all of the animals the sky the sun the moon and the stars.

Use your sense of taste and touch to truly interact and engage with your surroundings and ENJOY and savour each mouthful, each touch as you drink in the nectar of life, the divine energy. Use your sense of hearing to listen deeply to your own heart and allow your soul to speak loud and clear. Loose yourself in the intoxicating smells of a gorgeous hot bath filled essential oils such as lavender, rose and rosemary. Today, more than ever before, become aware of everything and anything inside and around you and let it fill you with a deep sense of gratitude and joy.

Let's start today by asking yourself: "what brings me joy"? Write down a list including people, activities, books, music, movies, travel, spaces and places etc etc write it all down! The key is to really listen to how these make you feel on the inside so stay focused and open as you perform this healing task setting yourself up for a successful day and life.

Now ask yourself " how can I bring more joy into my everyday life?

How can I find the beauty in the ordinary?"

Our life is made up from a collection of moments: ask yourself throughout your day how do I want to remember my life?

Which moments do you cherish the most? And do you manage to make time for them every single day?

Often we believe that in order to live a joyful life we must do something BIG, something extraordinary, however my love, as we just discovered: life is made up from every day moments! And the more you decide to plan your day in a way that feels joyful by adding in 5-20mins of what brings you joy here and there, the more life itself starts to appear JOYFUL to you: every day mondane life takes on a whole other meaning when you decide to add in a little sparkle here and there. And it all starts with YOU getting clear about what truly sparks joy and love for you. So commit to writing down your JOYLIST now! Remember, the only one who knows what truly brings you joy is YOU so getting clear on your joy is vital to living a successful, joyful life on all levels. Start now!

And after that?... you know it: it's time for your Morning Rituals:

Step 1 Space :

Go to your special place where you start YOUR day. Sitting down make yourself comfortable in the ways that you know best with your favourite scented candle, incense, music or nothing but sacred silence- up to you.

Step 2 Breathe & Check In:

Close your eyes (NOT NOW OBVS). Place your hands on your heart. Breathe in deeply "I see you", exhale "I love you". Repeat for 2mins.

Pay close attention to ALL that may come up for you: all that your feeling, thinking and sensing just invite it all to flow through you.

Then start to ask yourself as you inhale: "how do I feel"? As you exhale allow the answer to land. Continue here for another 5 breaths. Stay open to how the answer may arrive: an image, a colour, a feeling, a voice, a memory these are all valid and equally important for you today. Now that you know a little bit more about how you are actually feeling at this moment in time move your hands down to your stomach: breathe in "what do I need?" Exhale allow that answer to land, continue here for another 5 breaths.

Step 3 High Vibes :

Now that you know whats really going on, what dialogue your mind is currently listening to we can take mindful actions to FINETUNE your current mood into one of LOVE, EXPANSION and CELEBRATION. WHAT you say? Bare with me:

Think of someone you LOVE unconditionally (BIG points if it's yourself). Remember the colour of their eyes, the warm smile they always give you, their scent, the last time you saw them. What did you do together? What time of day was it? What season? What were YOU wearing? How did it feel when they hugged YOU? That wonderful nourishing feeling of love starting at the heart spreading down all the way through to the toes and down through the arms and hands. Listen to their words now as they tell you how much YOU mean to them. How YOU are an inspiration in their life, how just knowing that YOU are a part of them makes them swell with love and pride.... THATS it beauty... NOW YOU GOT IT.... stay there. Close your eyes fall in love...stay there. Deep breath in, feeling all this love swirling around inside of you, when you are ready to exhale send ALL of your love right back to them thanking them for being in your life.

Step 4 Day Planning / Intention Setting :

From this place of unconditional LOVE look at your day:

What simple steps can you make towards your dream today? Choose

3 things and write them here hehe yep YOU DECIDE which steps babe!! WHY YOU?!! Because YOU ARE THE ONLY ONE THAT KNOWS YOU! 123 GO:

1

2

3

Thats it!!! How simple was that? And it took you like 10mins???Out of your entire day!!

Now one tiny little thing and then your off;)

(Promise)!!

Step 5 Inspiration:

Write down your JOYLIST here! (and if you already did it write down your top 10 here):

1

2

3

4

5

6

7

8

9

10

Day 26 Believe

Good morning my love,

Today is such a special day, can you feel it too? There is just something about TODAY that makes me feel so incredibly happy!!!

I just KNOW in my heart, with every inch of my being, that TODAY is YOUR day gorgeous!! Today is the day you overcome all fears and doubts and start to 100% believe in yourself!

In your worthiness, your amazingness and in you ability to do, have and be anything you dream of!!!

Similarly to The law of manifestation so it is with BELIEF systems.

"He who says he can and he who says he can't are both usually right"

So my love what is it going to be? For far too long you have been telling yourself all the reasons for why your dreams haven't come true... For far too long you have been waiting for someone else to come along and lift you up and out of who you are. Saving you from yourself.

But my love, ONLY you can decide when it is time to RISE beyond the old limited beliefs that have kept you feeling trapped and small.

Are you ready NOW to finally FREE yourself? Are you ready NOW to take your seat on the throne that has been waiting for you for eons? Are you ready NOW to co-create, receive and live your wildest dream life????

However that may look? However that may feel?

Remember as a toddler you didn't know how to walk yet, however you had a firm believe that you would one day be walking and running around. There was NOTHING inside of you or around you that told you otherwise: and so you kept on practising every single day, because you not only believed, you KNEW in every cell of your being, that you were completely capable of achieving this dream.

SO WHAT CHANGED MY LOVE?

Let go of any voices in your head that says you can't. Instead REPLACE all of them with the one that says Hell yeah I CAN:)

Say "YES" with me RIGHT NOW my lovely, Shout YES JOSIE;

"Dear Universe I know you can hear me I am ready now to own my true power and to receive and achieve all of my most positive dreams' 'I BELIEVE in myself I BELIEVE in Life, I BELIEVE that I am destined for greatness and that it is my birthright to live my most beautiful radiant and fulfilling life Starting NOW NOW NOW"

And oh yes my love; indeed you are.

Xxxx Love you more than you will ever know xxxx Josephine

Step 1 Space :

Go to your special place where you start YOUR day. Sitting down make yourself comfortable in the ways that you know best with your favourite scented candle, incense, music or nothing but sacred silence- up to you.

Step 2 Breathe & Check In:

Close your eyes (NOT NOW OBVS). Place your hands on your heart. Breathe in deeply "I see you", exhale "I love you". Repeat for

2mins.

Pay close attention to ALL that may come up for you: all that your feeling, thinking and sensing just invite it all to flow through you.

Then start to ask yourself as you inhale: "how do I feel"? As you exhale allow the answer to land. Continue here for another 5 breaths. Stay open to how the answer may arrive: an image, a colour, a feeling, a voice, a memory these are all valid and equally important for you today. Now that you know a little bit more about how you are actually feeling at this moment in time move your hands down to your stomach: breathe in "what do I need?" Exhale allow that answer to land, continue here for another 5 breaths.

Step 3 High Vibes :

Now that you know whats really going on, what dialogue your mind is currently listening to we can take mindful actions to FINETUNE your current mood into one of LOVE, EXPANSION and CELEBRATION. WHAT you say? Bare with me:

Think of someone you LOVE unconditionally (BIG points if it's yourself). Remember the colour of their eyes, the warm smile they always give you, their scent, the last time you saw them. What did you do together? What time of day was it? What season? What were YOU wearing? How did it feel when they hugged YOU? That wonderful nourishing feeling of love starting at the heart spreading down all the way through to the toes and down through the arms and hands. Listen to their words now as they tell you how much YOU mean to them. How YOU are an inspiration in their life, how just knowing that YOU are a part of them makes them swell with love and pride.... THATS it beauty... NOW YOU GOT IT.... stay there. Close your eyes fall in love...stay there. Deep breath in, feeling all this love swirling around inside of you, when you are ready to exhale send ALL of your love right back to them thanking them for being in your life.

Step 4 Day Planning / Intention Setting :

From this place of unconditional LOVE look at your day:

What simple steps can you make towards your dream today? Choose 3 things and write them here hehe yep YOU DECIDE which steps babe!! WHY YOU?!! Because YOU ARE THE ONLY ONE THAT KNOWS YOU! 123 GO:

1

2

3

Thats it!!! How simple was that? And it took you like 10mins???Out of your entire day!!

Now one tiny little thing and then your off;)

(Promise)!!

Step 5 Inspiration:

I invite you to recall 3 times in your life where you put your mind to something, kept at it and 100% BELIEVED it would work out!! Write down now how it made you feel when you first started and what you did in order to keep on believing that it would all be OK ie that the Universe was looking after you and that the two of you were co creating together to make this wish come true.

1

2

3

Day 27 You have found it

Cherished one, welcome to day 27!! Take a moment to recognize the gravity of this statement: for 27days, every single morning- whether you felt like it or not- YOU decided to make time for YOU. YOU decided to start your day in the most elevating way: heightening and brightening your energy of mind body and spirit. Every single morning you got clearer and clearer about who you are becoming, and who you no longer wish to be. Every day you attracted more and more positive energy including people, ideas, wealth and health into your being, and because of this you are now where you are: grounded and rooted in yourself, in your success of living a beautiful, balanced life in full alignment with who you are, and who you came here to be.

So my love, take this moment to simply contemplate your success. Due to your commitment and your desire to transform you HAVE and are still transforming!!!

Take a moment to recall all the ways your life has changed so far... perhaps your energy levels have increased and you no longer feel the afternoon dip so badly? Perhaps you have started and committed to following a healthy exercise and eating routine? Perhaps you feel closer now to knowing how living your truth each and every day looks and feels like for you? Perhaps something ended during this period: Perhaps you were finally ready to take that leap of faith and leave whatever was no longer serving you- a partner, a habit, a job etc?

One thing I am sure of: *"YOU HAVE FOUND THAT SPARK THAT YOU WERE LOOKING FOR"*

And how do I know that you ask?

Because otherwise you would simply not be here with me again today!!! You are here, and have continued to be here every single day because YOU, yourself as much as everyone else around you, are NOTICING and RECOGNIZING the transformation. However subtle or evident you may feel it, you are here because you are witnessing the magic: life at work. You co creating with the Universe. And that my love is the key to your unlocking, of living your most authentic, radiant, magical, wildest dreams kinda life yeahhhhh!!!!

Spend the next few moments noticing how your body is receiving the breath, the nectar of life.... Notice how your entire body including mind, body and soul, all of your cells are gracefully taking in this divine energy so effortlessly and gracefully. 4 weeks ago your body took in only 25% of the oxygen that is now filling your body. Why? What changed? YOU DID MY LOVE. YOU DID.

When we finally awaken to our true power, our ability to transform and transcend whatever limited beliefs which have kept us small we start to breathe in life in a whole other way. Our very way of living changes as we communion with the Earth, the sun the moon and the stars. With life itself. Have a wonderful day my love, enjoy every bit of the journey...

Love you xx Josephine

Enjoy your beautiful energising Morning Rituals:

Step 1 Space :

Go to your special place where you start YOUR day. Sitting down make yourself comfortable in the ways that you know best with your favourite scented candle, incense, music or nothing but sacred silence- up to you.

Step 2 Breathe & Check In:

Close your eyes (NOT NOW OBVS). Place your hands on your heart. Breathe in deeply "I see you", exhale "I love you". Repeat for 2mins.

Pay close attention to ALL that may come up for you: all that your feeling, thinking and sensing just invite it all to flow through you.

Then start to ask yourself as you inhale: "how do I feel"? As you exhale allow the answer to land. Continue here for another 5 breaths. Stay open to how the answer may arrive: an image, a colour, a feeling, a voice, a memory these are all valid and equally important for you today. Now that you know a little bit more about how you are actually feeling at this moment in time move your hands down to your stomach: breathe in "what do I need?" Exhale allow that answer to land, continue here for another 5 breaths.

Step 3 High Vibes :

Now that you know whats really going on, what dialogue your mind is currently listening to we can take mindful actions to FINETUNE your current mood into one of LOVE, EXPANSION and CELEBRATION. WHAT you say? Bare with me:

Think of someone you LOVE unconditionally (BIG points if it's yourself). Remember the colour of their eyes, the warm smile they always give you, their scent, the last time you saw them. What did you do together? What time of day was it? What season? What were YOU wearing? How did it feel when they hugged YOU? That wonderful nourishing feeling of love starting at the heart spreading down all the way through to the toes and down through the arms and hands. Listen to their words now as they tell you how much YOU mean to them. How YOU are an inspiration in their life, how just knowing that YOU are a part of them makes them swell with love and pride.... THATS it beauty... NOW YOU GOT IT.... stay there. Close your eyes fall in love...stay there. Deep breath in, feeling all this love swirling around inside of you, when you are ready to exhale send ALL of your love right back to them thanking them for being in your life.

Step 4 Day Planning / Intention Setting :

From this place of unconditional LOVE look at your day:

What simple steps can you make towards your dream today? Choose 3 things and write them here hehe yep YOU DECIDE which steps babe!! WHY YOU?!! Because YOU ARE THE ONLY ONE THAT KNOWS YOU! 123 GO:

1

2

3

Step 5 Inspiration:

Write down all the ways being part of The 30 Day Morning Miracle has transformed your life. Think about yourself as the multi dimensional being that you are (mental, emotional, physical and spiritual- all levels and areas of your existence which has changed, remember everything is connected so when we change in one area all the others are affected too:).

1

2

3

4

5

6

7

8

9

10

Day 28 Flow with life

Good morning gorgeous soul,

Extend your arms out to the sides and say with me now:

" I welcome in positive energy into my heart. I give thanks for all that I am and all that I am becoming. I now totally release everything and anything that has held me back in the past and they are forgiven and free and so am I. I flow easily with life. Life carries me and life supports my every dream and desire. I remember NOW and forever more that impossible broken down says I Am Possible".

Take a deep breath in as we welcome in this glowing energy life force and as you exhale empty every last bit of negativity, heaviness and doubt.

Continue to focus on your breath as you hear the following words:

I NOW commit to flowing with life.

I NOW surrender all of my worries to the Universe

I NOW surrender all of the dreams to the Universe

I NOW dare to dream big

I NOW pledge to live my life in the ways that I planned to when I first came to be

I NOW live my fullest most wonderful, balanced, healthy, wealthy happy life.

I NOW gracefully RECEIVE life as the gift that it is and I promise to treat it as such.

I NOW allow others to help support me, on all levels, in all areas of my life.

I NOW say YES to love, to life, to the Universe itself.

I NOW devout my entire mind, body and soul to becoming the vessel of love and light that I was born to be, and invite the Universe to do it's magnificent work through me.

I NOW step out of the way and simply BECOME ME.

I NOW AM whole, loved and alive and so it is.....

Always and forever

Thank you, Thank you, Thank you

Breathe in trust, exhale fear.

Today my love, more than ever before DECIDE to step into your true power which is LOVE, INTUITION and HIGHER SEEING (the ability to see everything and everyone including yourself from a higher perspective).

I have sooo much faith in YOU,

Love xx Josephine

Step 1 Space :

Go to your special place where you start YOUR day. Sitting down make yourself comfortable in the ways that you know best with your favourite scented candle, incense, music or nothing but sacred silence- up to you.

Step 2 Breathe & Check In:

Close your eyes (NOT NOW OBVS). Place your hands on your

heart. Breathe in deeply "I see you", exhale "I love you". Repeat for 2mins.

Pay close attention to ALL that may come up for you: all that your feeling, thinking and sensing just invite it all to flow through you.

Then start to ask yourself as you inhale: "how do I feel"? As you exhale allow the answer to land. Continue here for another 5 breaths. Stay open to how the answer may arrive: an image, a colour, a feeling, a voice, a memory these are all valid and equally important for you today. Now that you know a little bit more about how you are actually feeling at this moment in time move your hands down to your stomach: breathe in "what do I need?" Exhale allow that answer to land, continue here for another 5 breaths.

Step 3 High Vibes :

Now that you know whats really going on, what dialogue your mind is currently listening to we can take mindful actions to FINETUNE your current mood into one of LOVE, EXPANSION and CELEBRATION. WHAT you say? Bare with me:

Think of someone you LOVE unconditionally (BIG points if it's yourself). Remember the colour of their eyes, the warm smile they always give you, their scent, the last time you saw them. What did you do together? What time of day was it? What season? What were YOU wearing? How did it feel when they hugged YOU? That wonderful nourishing feeling of love starting at the heart spreading down all the way through to the toes and down through the arms and hands. Listen to their words now as they tell you how much YOU mean to them. How YOU are an inspiration in their life, how just knowing that YOU are a part of them makes them swell with love and pride.... THATS it beauty... NOW YOU GOT IT.... stay there. Close your eyes fall in love...stay there. Deep breath in, feeling all this love swirling around inside of you, when you are ready to exhale send ALL of your love right back to them thanking them for being in your life.

Step 4 Day Planning / Intention Setting :

From this place of unconditional LOVE look at your day:

What simple steps can you make towards your dream today? Choose 3 things and write them here hehe yep YOU DECIDE which steps babe!! WHY YOU?!! Because YOU ARE THE ONLY ONE THAT KNOWS YOU! 123 GO:

1

2

3

Thats it!!! How simple was that? And it took you like 10mins???Out of your entire day!!

Now one tiny little thing and then your off;)

(Promise)!!

Step 5 Inspiration:

Ask yourself: where can I flow easily with life? In what areas of my life do I want to find a little more ease and balance? Where am I ready to give up the need to control?

1

2

3

4

5

Day 29 Journey

Dear heart,

A new day has come upon us; yet again the sun has risen and we feel her warmth healing our bodies and minds.

Enjoy these first few moments of the day, cherish the dawn of the day, loose yourself in the silence, allowing this peaceful energy to guide you back into your heart realigning you with what truly matters to you in this life time...

Today I invite you to remember that life is always about the journey: the becoming. Through the darkness and the light we rise. Throughout our life.

It is said that it is through our shadow that we find our light: that the only way to gain true self acceptance and confidence we must journey through. Not up or down or around but gather our courage to simply go right through the middle, facing our deepest fears and surrendering our ego and our pride.

On this special morning I ask you to perform the following ritual: placing your left hand on your heart and your right hand out in front of you away from the body, repeating these words:

"From the Universe I receive, to the Earth I give back. For myself I keep nothing"

Continue to repeat these powerful words and say them with confidence and love.

"From the Universe I receive, to the Earth I give back. For myself I keep nothing."

"From the Universe I receive, to the Earth I give back. For myself I keep nothing."

"From the Universe I receive, to the Earth I give back. For myself I keep nothing."

"From the Universe I receive, to the Earth I give back. For myself I keep nothing."

"From the Universe I receive, to the Earth I give back. For myself I keep nothing."

Through this ritual you are emptying out any fears of lack, any desire to hold onto love or control. Through these words you are confirming to yourself and the Universe that Abundance is your natural state: the natural state of the Universe is Abundance. So you never need to hoard any feelings, energies, people, belongings, beliefs etc and through this process, this journey of letting go, you are recognising and declaring yourself a vessel, a vehicle for the Universe to work through and with. YOU are a light worker my love, otherwise you would not be here with me again today!!!

Let's give thanks for all that you have, and all that you are becoming: be a traveller of your own life's story. Be the hero/heroine of your own adventure.

Enjoy the journey for THAT is what makes up our life!!! And it is only through the journeying that we realize the magnificent beings that we truly are.

You are the Universe and the Universe is YOU.

Love and celebrate my love xxxx Josephine

Step 1 Space :

Go to your special place where you start YOUR day. Sitting down make yourself comfortable in the ways that you know best with your favourite scented candle, incense, music or nothing but sacred silence- up to you.

Step 2 Breathe & Check In:

Close your eyes (NOT NOW OBVS). Place your hands on your heart. Breathe in deeply "I see you", exhale "I love you". Repeat for 2mins.

Pay close attention to ALL that may come up for you: all that your feeling, thinking and sensing just invite it all to flow through you.

Then start to ask yourself as you inhale: "how do I feel"? As you exhale allow the answer to land. Continue here for another 5 breaths. Stay open to how the answer may arrive: an image, a colour, a feeling, a voice, a memory these are all valid and equally important for you today. Now that you know a little bit more about how you are actually feeling at this moment in time move your hands down to your stomach: breathe in "what do I need?" Exhale allow that answer to land, continue here for another 5 breaths.

Step 3 High Vibes :

Now that you know whats really going on, what dialogue your mind is currently listening to we can take mindful actions to FINETUNE your current mood into one of LOVE, EXPANSION and CELEBRATION. WHAT you say? Bare with me:

Think of someone you LOVE unconditionally (BIG points if it's yourself). Remember the colour of their eyes, the warm smile they always give you, their scent, the last time you saw them. What did you do together? What time of day was it? What season? What were YOU wearing? How did it feel when they hugged YOU? That wonderful nourishing feeling of love starting at the heart spreading down all the way through to the toes and down through the arms and hands. Listen to their words now as they tell you how much YOU mean to them. How YOU are an inspiration in their life, how just knowing that YOU are a part of them makes them swell with love and pride.... THATS it beauty... NOW YOU GOT IT.... stay there. Close your eyes fall in love...stay there. Deep breath in, feeling all this love swirling around inside of you, when you are ready to exhale send ALL of your love right back to them thanking them for being in your life.

Step 4 Day Planning / Intention Setting :

From this place of unconditional LOVE look at your day:

What simple steps can you make towards your dream today? Choose 3 things and write them here hehe yep YOU DECIDE which steps babe!! WHY YOU?!! Because YOU ARE THE ONLY ONE THAT KNOWS YOU! 123 GO:

1

2

3

Step 5 Inspiration:

I invite you to visualise YOUR IDEAL happy life and focus on how it makes you feel in the body. Do this with your eyes closed so your HEART and soul have space to speak.

Write down 3 things such as feelings, sensations and images that come up for you during this visualisation:

1

2

3

Day 30 Home Coming: You are the miracle

Good morning beautiful being of love and light, welcome to this incredible new day:

"Welcome HOME my love"

Today marks the day of your final transformation: today you can turn around and say "I did it"!! For 30 days and 30 nights YOU stayed true to your dreams, to your goals, to everything that makes your heart and your soul sing!

And though there might have been many times where your mind doubted and told you all the reasons for why you shouln't/didn't need to make this space for yourself and yet somehow, something kept you coming back for more!!!!

WHY?

Because YOU were ready for this big change.

Because YOUR soul was fed up not being heard.

Because YOUR body wanted real nourishment and movement.

Because YOUR mind wanted to be challenged and fully utilise its incredible potential

Because YOUR heart had been calling me into being: ready to be guided back home

Because the Universe needs YOU now more than ever before

Because YOU have something special to gift to this new world that is emerging

My love, the truth is that through the past 30 days you have been challenged and tested in all sorts of ways for all sorts of different reasons but more than anything: you have been challenged in order for you to fully awaken to the only truth that ever existed across all planes and throughout time and space.

YOU ARE THE MIRACLE.

WHAT YOU SEEK IS ALSO SEEKING YOU

THE UNIVERSE LIVES AND BREATHS, DANCES AND CO CREATES WITH YOU, AT ALL TIMES (EVEN NOW NOW NOW!!:)

YOU HAVE ARRIVED HOME NOW! FINALLY! BECAUSE YOU RECOGNISE THIS TRUTH

YOU ARE WHERE YOU ARE NOW BECAUSE YOU ARE READY FOR WHATEVER COMES YOUR WAY: SEEEING EACH LESSON IN LIFE AS THE BLESSING IT IS

YOU ARE WHERE YOU ARE BECAUSE YOU READY FOR THE NEXT EMBODIMENT IN THIS ETERNAL JOURNEY OF THE SOUL

YOU ARE THE CREATOR, THE DESTROYER, THE HEALER, THE WATER AND THE FIRE, THE EARTH THE SUN THE MOON AND THE STARS

EVERYTHING YOU SEE IS BUT A REFLECTION OF YOUR OWN FREQUENCY

YOU CREATE UNIVERSES WITH YOUR WORDS

YOUR WORDS ARE YOUR PRAYERS

YOUR THOUGHTS ARE YOUR POWERTOOLS

YOUR AWARENESS CHANGES EVERYTHING

YOU, AND ONLY YOU, HOLD THE KEYS TO YOUR SUCCESS ON ALL LEVELS

NOW GO LIVE

From my heart to yours my love, I shall miss you but I know we will meet again:

"What was once created in love shall never cease to exist"

Love you always, xxxx Josephine

For the last time together with me, let's do your Morning Rituals:

Step 1 Space :

Go to your special place where you start YOUR day. Sitting down make yourself comfortable in the ways that you know best with your favourite scented candle, incense, music or nothing but sacred silence- up to you.

Step 2 Breathe & Check In:

Close your eyes (NOT NOW OBVS). Place your hands on your heart. Breathe in deeply "I see you", exhale "I love you". Repeat for 2mins.

Pay close attention to ALL that may come up for you: all that your feeling, thinking and sensing just invite it all to flow through you.

Then start to ask yourself as you inhale: "how do I feel"? As you exhale allow the answer to land. Continue here for another 5 breaths. Stay open to how the answer may arrive: an image, a colour, a feeling, a voice, a memory these are all valid and equally important for you today. Now that you know a little bit more about how you are actually feeling at this moment in time move your hands down to

your stomach: breathe in "what do I need?" Exhale allow that answer to land, continue here for another 5 breaths.

Step 3 High Vibes :

Now that you know whats really going on, what dialogue your mind is currently listening to we can take mindful actions to FINETUNE your current mood into one of LOVE, EXPANSION and CELEBRATION. WHAT you say? Bare with me:

Think of someone you LOVE unconditionally (BIG points if it's yourself). Remember the colour of their eyes, the warm smile they always give you, their scent, the last time you saw them. What did you do together? What time of day was it? What season? What were YOU wearing? How did it feel when they hugged YOU? That wonderful nourishing feeling of love starting at the heart spreading down all the way through to the toes and down through the arms and hands. Listen to their words now as they tell you how much YOU mean to them. How YOU are an inspiration in their life, how just knowing that YOU are a part of them makes them swell with love and pride.... THATS it beauty... NOW YOU GOT IT.... stay there. Close your eyes fall in love...stay there. Deep breath in, feeling all this love swirling around inside of you, when you are ready to exhale send ALL of your love right back to them thanking them for being in your life.

Step 4 Day Planning / Intention Setting :

From this place of unconditional LOVE look at your day:

What simple steps can you make towards your dream today? Choose 3 things and write them here hehe yep YOU DECIDE which steps babe!! WHY YOU?!! Because YOU ARE THE ONLY ONE THAT KNOWS YOU! 123 GO:

1

2

3

Thats it!!! How simple was that? And it took you like 10mins???Out of your entire day!!

Now one tiny little thing and then your off;)

(Promise)!!

Step 5 Inspiration:

Looking forward into your NEW CHAPTER what teachings will you bring with you? What did The 30 Day Morning Miracle help you unravel about YOU? How can YOU make a difference to this new world this is emerging by being even more YOU? Write down your ideas below, then sign this final page and go out there and celebrate YOU. You made it my love, you are finally home: Having realized that you are the miracle!!!

1

2

3

4

5

6

7

8

9

10

Final words

Thank you from my heart for being here. Your existence means the world to me and to the evolution of our world as we know it.

It is my greatest hope that all of your dreams come true because I know YOU have everything you need with you now: you have it with you in your heart, in your mind, and in your soul that knows you better than any.

I pray you stay connected to your heart and that some of these Morning Rituals might be included in your own on going morning routine to help you check back in... so you always find your way back home.

"Remember my love, our true home is where our heart is"

Share your light with the world and share these teachings, whichever you found the most useful with all of your loved ones: every day ask yourself "what do I need to hear today" Then go out there and tell that to someone else.

Together we rise in love.

What you seek is also seeking
you

You are the miracle

Shine

CSB185082-1
This book was created at solentro.co.uk
The responsible publisher is Josephine McGrail.

Printed in Great Britain
by Amazon

80327113R00078